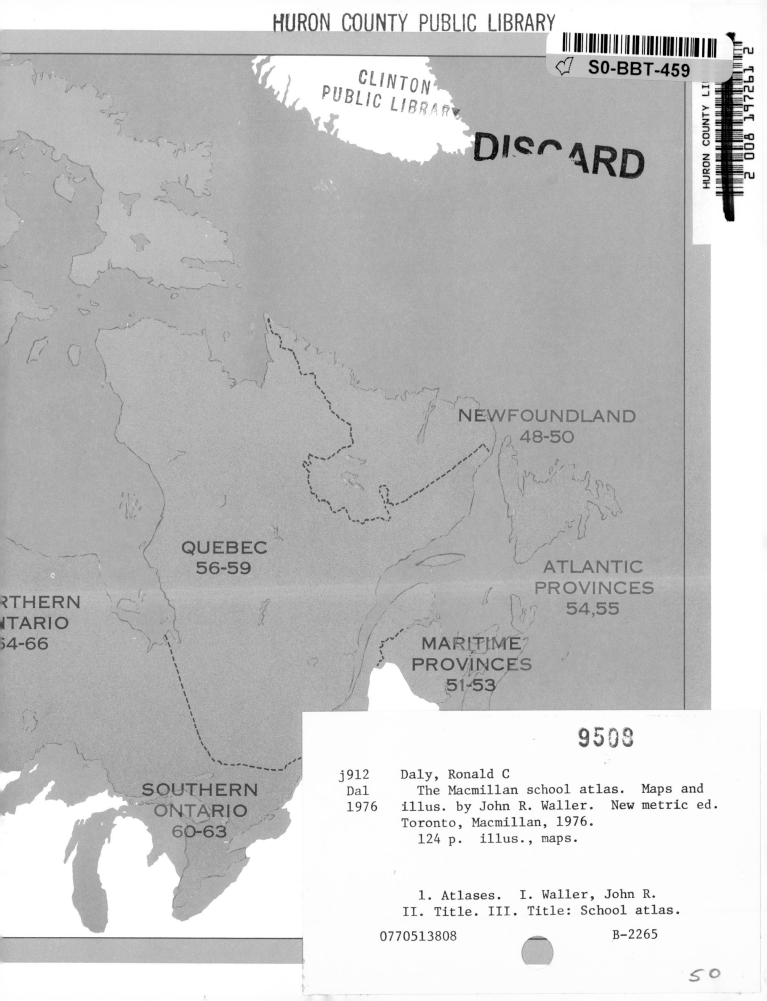

NEWFOUNDLAND
48-50

QUEBEC
56-59

ATLANTIC
PROVINCES
54,55

RTHERN
NTARIO
64-66

MARITIME
PROVINCES
51-53

SOUTHERN
ONTARIO
60-63

The Macmillan School Atlas

The Macmillan

SCHOOL ATLAS

New Metric Edition

RONALD C. DALY, B.A., M.Ed.

Principal, Fairmount Park Senior School, Toronto
Formerly Social Studies Consultant, Toronto Board of Education

Maps and illustrations by

JOHN R. WALLER

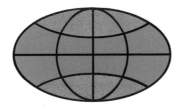

THE MACMILLAN COMPANY OF CANADA LIMITED

TORONTO

Acknowledgements

The author wishes to thank John Waller for his suggestions and skill in preparing the maps, and the editorial staff of the Macmillan Company of Canada for their assistance in planning and supervising the production of this new metric edition of the Atlas.

NOTE TO THE 1976 METRIC EDITION

In this new edition of the Macmillan School Atlas all measurements have been changed to SI units and all the maps have been updated to reflect the many changes that have been taking place in recent years in the political make-up of our world. The map of Canada's Northland has been completely redrawn and new maps on North American land use, South American rainfall, average temperatures, and vegetation, native peoples in North America in 1500 and in Canada today, areas of colonial influence in North America in 1664, and the political development of Canada have been added. The explanatory notes at the beginning of the book have been revised, with new material on map projections being included.

© 1976 THE MACMILLAN COMPANY OF CANADA LIMITED, 70 BOND STREET, TORONTO M5B 1X3. AFFILIATED WITH MACLEAN-HUNTER LEARNING MATERIALS COMPANY.

ISBN 0-7705-1380-8

Printed in Canada

Contents

The World

Man has known for many years that the planet on which he lives is a sphere. Although maps can tell us much about its surface, only a globe can show correctly the size, shape, and position of the different areas of land and water.

The distance round the earth is 40 075 kilometres. This is slightly more than 7 times the distance across Canada.

The earth's diameter at the equator is 12 757 km. The diameter from north to south is 12 713 km.

The world is not perfectly round but is slightly flattened at the poles. However, since this flattening is so slight and since the earth is so large, we may well think of it as having more or less the shape of a ball.

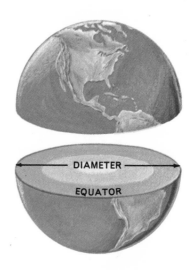

Hemispheres

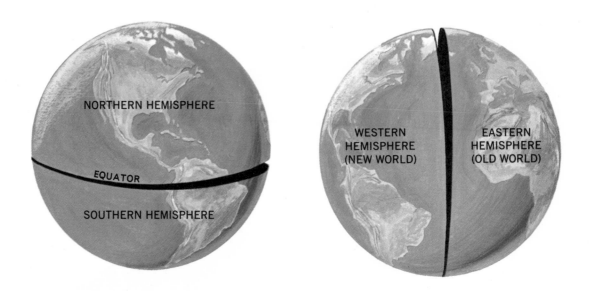

When we look at a globe we see only half of it at one time. This is called a *hemisphere,* which means "half a sphere". No matter how a globe is held, it will show that the earth is divided into two hemispheres, the half that you see and the half that you do not see. These two hemispheres are opposite each other, and by placing them together we are able to make a whole sphere.

By dividing the earth in two at different places we get many different hemispheres. For example, if we cut the earth along the equator, we would separate it into the *Northern Hemisphere* and the *Southern Hemisphere*. If we divided the earth through the Atlantic and Pacific oceans into the Old World and the New World, we would separate it into the *Eastern Hemisphere* and the *Western Hemisphere*.

Two other important hemispheres are the *Land Hemisphere* and the *Water Hemisphere*. The Land Hemisphere contains over ninety per cent of all the land on the earth's surface.

LAND HEMISPHERE

WATER HEMISPHERE

Great Circles

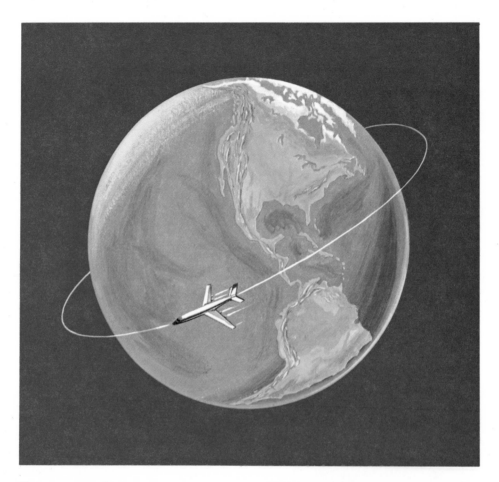

From any place we can draw a circle round the earth that will divide the earth into two hemispheres. Such a line is called a *great circle.*

The shortest distance between any two places on the earth is found on the great circle that joins these two places together. This is called the *great-circle distance.*

Many ships have tried to follow great-circle routes but have found it impossible because of land obstacles. Airplanes can more easily follow these routes unless they are forbidden to do so for political reasons.

10

Latitude

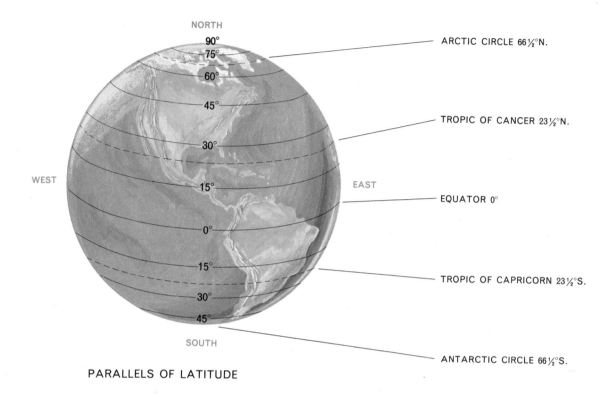

NORTH

90°
75°
60°
45°
30°
15°
0°
15°
30°
45°

SOUTH

WEST

EAST

ARCTIC CIRCLE 66½°N.

TROPIC OF CANCER 23½°N.

EQUATOR 0°

TROPIC OF CAPRICORN 23½°S.

ANTARCTIC CIRCLE 66½°S.

PARALLELS OF LATITUDE

Any circle can be divided into a number of equal distances known as *degrees*. Every circle, no matter how large or small, has 360 of these degrees. Therefore in half a circle (a hemisphere) there are 180 degrees (180°).

The most important dividing line going round the earth from east to west is the *equator*. The position of this imaginary line round the middle of the earth is shown on the globe and is 0° *latitude*. Other lines can be drawn from east to west, parallel to the equator. These lines are called *parallels of latitude*. All places on the same parallel of latitude are an equal distance from the equator. Places north of the equator are in the north latitudes and places south of the equator are in the south latitudes.

11

The numbers on the parallels stand for degrees of latitude. Distance from the equator may be measured in these degrees. No place on the earth's surface can have a latitude greater than 90°. The latitude at the north pole is 90° north of the equator. What would the latitude at the south pole be?

One degree of latitude is equal to about 113 km. Knowing this we can find the distance of any place from the equator if we have its

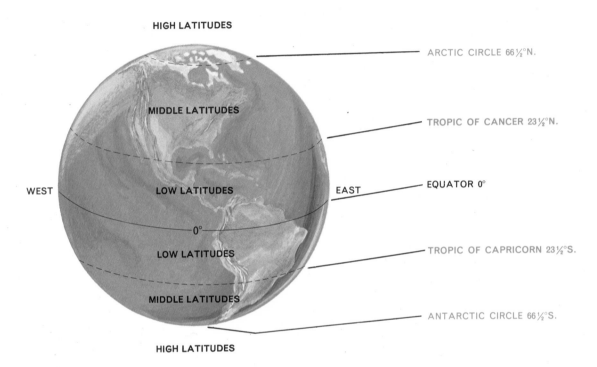

latitude. All places on the same parallel are directly east or west of each other. Because of this, the parallels of latitude can help us to find directions as well as distances.

Using parallels of latitude we can divide the earth into *Low Latitudes, Middle Latitudes,* and *High Latitudes.* Zones can be helpful when comparing climates on various parts of the earth's surface. However, you must consider other factors that influence climate before making general statements about a particular place.

12

Longitude

MERIDIANS OF LONGITUDE

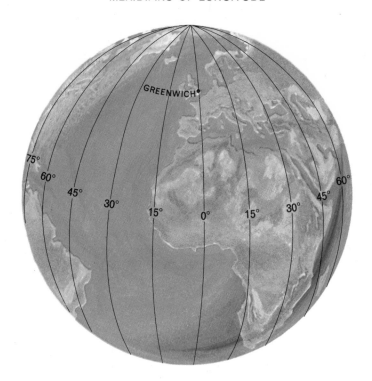

To help further in locating places on the earth's surface, a second set of imaginary lines can be drawn. These run from the north pole to the south pole and are called *meridians of longitude*.

Unlike the parallels of latitude, meridians are not parallel to one another but meet at two points—the north pole and the south pole. These lines show direction north and south.

The meridian that passes through Greenwich, a suburb of London, England, is 0° and is called the *prime meridian*.

The parallels of latitude and the meridians of longitude appear on most maps and globes as a network of lines, or *grid*. With this grid we can locate accurately any place on earth. We can also compare areas of the earth's surface with the same area on a globe.

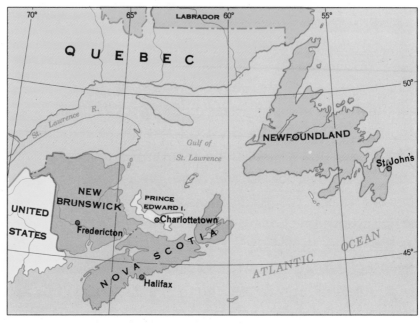

14

Maps

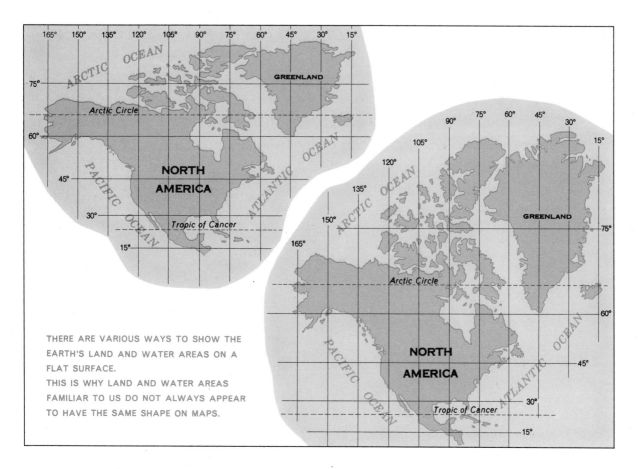

THERE ARE VARIOUS WAYS TO SHOW THE
EARTH'S LAND AND WATER AREAS ON A
FLAT SURFACE.
THIS IS WHY LAND AND WATER AREAS
FAMILIAR TO US DO NOT ALWAYS APPEAR
TO HAVE THE SAME SHAPE ON MAPS.

A *map* is a picture of the earth or a part of its surface as seen from
above. With the exception of a globe, most maps show the features
of the earth on a flat surface. We know that a globe gives us the
truest picture of the outline of land and water on the earth's surface, but it is not always as easy to use and handle as a map is.
Map-makers have tried different ways of drawing the rounded
surface of the earth on a flat piece of paper, but they have always
found that they must make some changes in the distances or in
the size and shape of the earth's features. A map showing a large
area of the earth's surface has more distortion in some of its parts
than a map of only a small area.

15

Map-makers use *projections* to draw maps. A projection is a method of flattening the rounded surface of the earth so that it can be drawn on a sheet of paper. To draw a map, the map-maker must transfer the shapes of areas and the grid lines from the globe to the paper. Imagine a sheet of paper placed around a globe and a light placed inside the globe. The light shines through the globe and casts shadows of the outlines of the earth's features and the grid lines onto the paper. By tracing these shadows a map is prepared. More complicated projections are not prepared in this way but are the result of careful mathematical calculations that show how the meridians and parallels should be spaced.

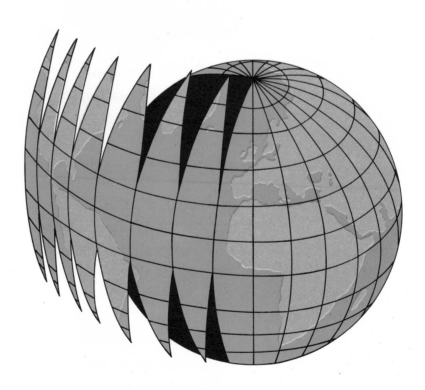

These diagrams show three ways in which the rounded surface of the earth can be represented on a flat surface. In each case the shapes of some areas and some distances are not the same as they are on the globe. If you examine the world maps on pages 26-33, you will see how these distortions appear on different maps.

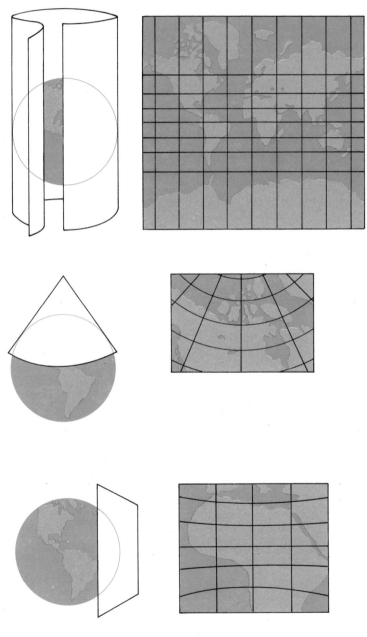

The Legend and the Scale

⊙ • CITIES, TOWNS	✈ AIRPORTS	LUMBERING
═══ ROADS	OIL	PULP AND PAPER
┼─┼─┼ RAILWAYS	MINING	GAS
BOUNDARIES	POWER SITES	REFINERY

Maps are usually grouped according to the kind of information they give. Several kinds of information may be combined on one map.

Many features on a map are shown by special *symbols* and by colours. These are explained in the *legend* of the map. The legend also usually gives the *title* of the map and the *scale*. Every map has its own symbols and colouring. What is used on one map is not always used on another. Colouring in particular often has different meanings. To understand a map we must read it carefully. One of the first steps in map-reading is to look at the legend to see what the symbols mean.

BAR OR GRAPHIC SCALE

0 1000 2000	1 cm = 500 km
0 200 400	1 cm = 100 km
0 50 100 150 200	1 cm = 50 km

The scale indicates the size of the area shown on the map. In the legend of most maps there is a *bar*, or *graphic*, scale divided into sections. By comparing distances measured on the map with this scale, we can tell what the distances are on the earth.

Each division represents a certain number of kilometres. On different maps the same length of line can stand for different distances. On one map 1 cm might represent 100 km; on another map it might stand for only 50 km.

18

The Direction Sign

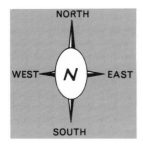

Most maps have a key for finding direction. This is usually an arrow that points toward the north. You must remember, however, that due north is not always at the top of the map.

Elevation

Look at the picture at the right. You can see that the land is not the same everywhere. Some places are only a little above the level of the ocean. These areas are called *lowlands*. Other areas are higher above the ocean level and are called *highlands*.

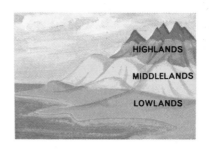

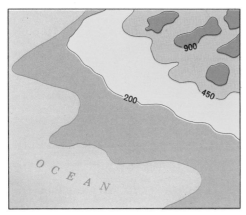

At the left you see a map of the same area. Lines are drawn on the map to join together places where the height of the land is the same. Notice that all the places where the land is 200 m above the level of the ocean are joined together by a line.

All the land that is between 0 and 200 m above sea level is coloured green. The land from 200 m to 450 m is coloured yellow. The land from 450 m to 900 m above sea level is coloured brown. What colour is used to show the land over 900 m?

Night and Day

Once a day the earth makes one complete turn from west to east. It turns round an imaginary line that passes through the centre of the earth from the north pole to the south pole. This line is known as the *axis* of the earth.

We depend on the sun for our heat and our light. As the earth spins on its axis, the part that faces the sun receives heat and light. It is *day* in this part of the earth. The part that is turned away from the sun is cool and is in darkness. It is *night* in this part of the earth.

As we watch the sun in the morning, we say it "rises" in the east. This is not so. The sun does not change its position at all. It is because the earth is turning from west to east that we see the sun "rise" in the east. Our last view of the sun is in the west, as the earth turns away from it.

Time

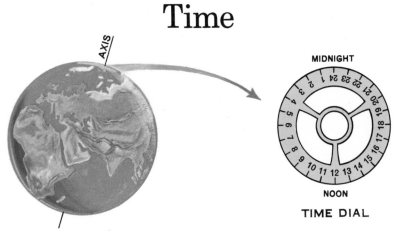

TIME DIAL

All places on Earth do not have noon at the same time. This is due to the earth's shape and to its spinning on its axis. In one day the earth completes one spin (rotation). In twenty-four hours it travels 360 degrees—15 degrees each hour. Noon where you live would be one hour later than in a place fifteen degrees east of you.

To avoid the confusion there would be if every place used its own time, *time zones* have been established. All places within a time zone have the same time. There are twenty-four of these time zones—one for every fifteen degrees.

The borders of time zones do not always follow meridians, but often follow the borders of countries or of provinces and states.

Canada's seven time zones are shown on the map below.

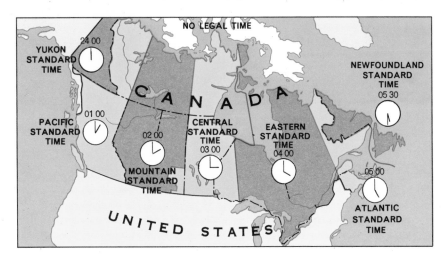

21

The Change of Seasons

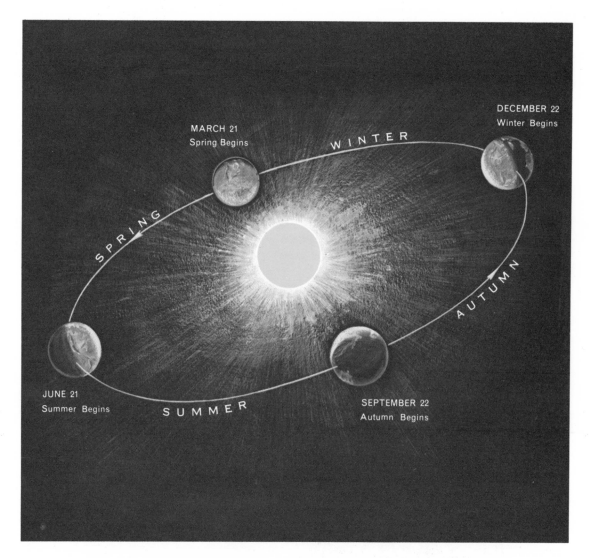

As the earth is turning on its axis, it is also revolving round the sun, in an *orbit*. At the same time, the axis of the earth always points to the North Star. This causes changes in the length of time various places on the earth receive sunlight. It also causes changes in the amount of heat these places receive.

This change in heating is called the change of the *seasons*.

The Earth and the Moon

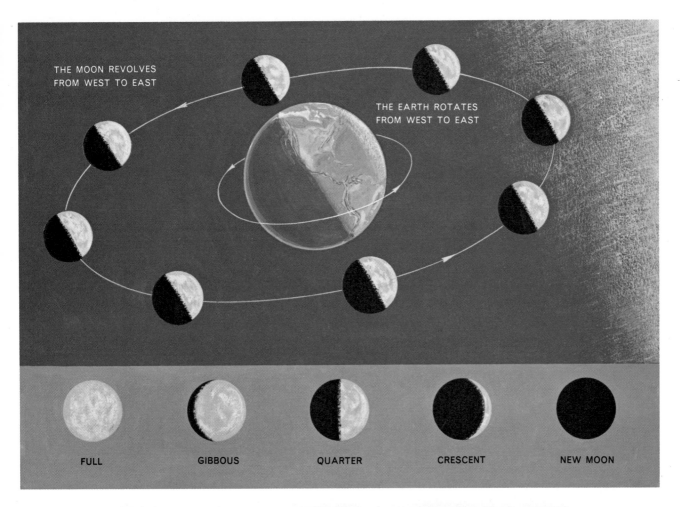

THE MOON REVOLVES FROM WEST TO EAST

THE EARTH ROTATES FROM WEST TO EAST

FULL   GIBBOUS   QUARTER   CRESCENT   NEW MOON

The *moon* is the brightest object in our night sky. To a person observing it from the earth, it seems to be as large as the sun. Actually it appears large only because it is closer to us than the sun. The distance from the earth to the moon is about 384 400 km. This is almost 10 times the distance round the earth at its equator.

If you observe the moon closely, you will see that it travels round the earth from west to east. As it does, the amount of it we see lighted changes. These changes are called *phases*.

23

24

GEOGRAPHIC TERMS

THIS IS A VIEW OF AN AREA THAT INCLUDES THE MAIN FEATURES FOUND ON THE EARTH'S SURFACE; THE GEOGRAPHIC TERMS ARE MARKED ON THESE.

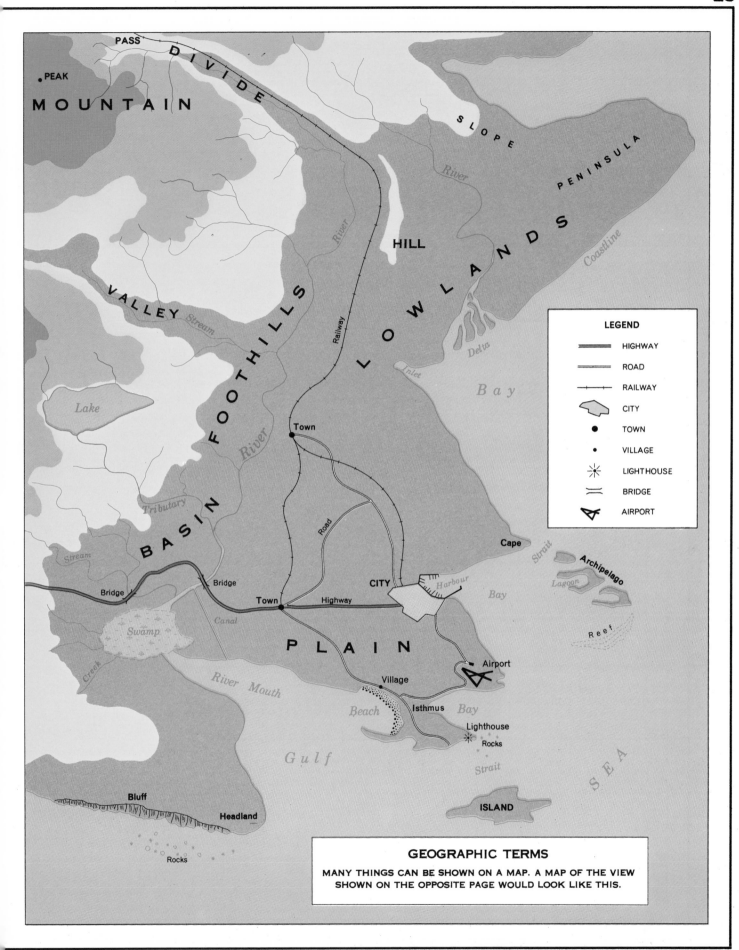

PASS

DIVIDE

• PEAK

M O U N T A I N

SLOPE

River

PENINSULA

HILL

L O W L A N D S

Coastline

VALLEY

Stream

River

Railway

Delta

Inlet

Lake

F O O T H I L L S

Bay

Town

River

Tributary

Road

LEGEND

HIGHWAY

ROAD

RAILWAY

CITY

TOWN

VILLAGE

LIGHTHOUSE

BRIDGE

AIRPORT

B A S I N

Stream

Cape

Strait

Archipelago

Lagoon

Bridge

Bridge

CITY

Harbour

Bay

Reef

Town

Highway

Canal

P L A I N

Swamp

Airport

Creek

River Mouth

Village

Beach

Isthmus

Bay

Lighthouse

Rocks

Gulf

Strait

S E A

Bluff

Headland

ISLAND

Rocks

GEOGRAPHIC TERMS

MANY THINGS CAN BE SHOWN ON A MAP. A MAP OF THE VIEW
SHOWN ON THE OPPOSITE PAGE WOULD LOOK LIKE THIS.

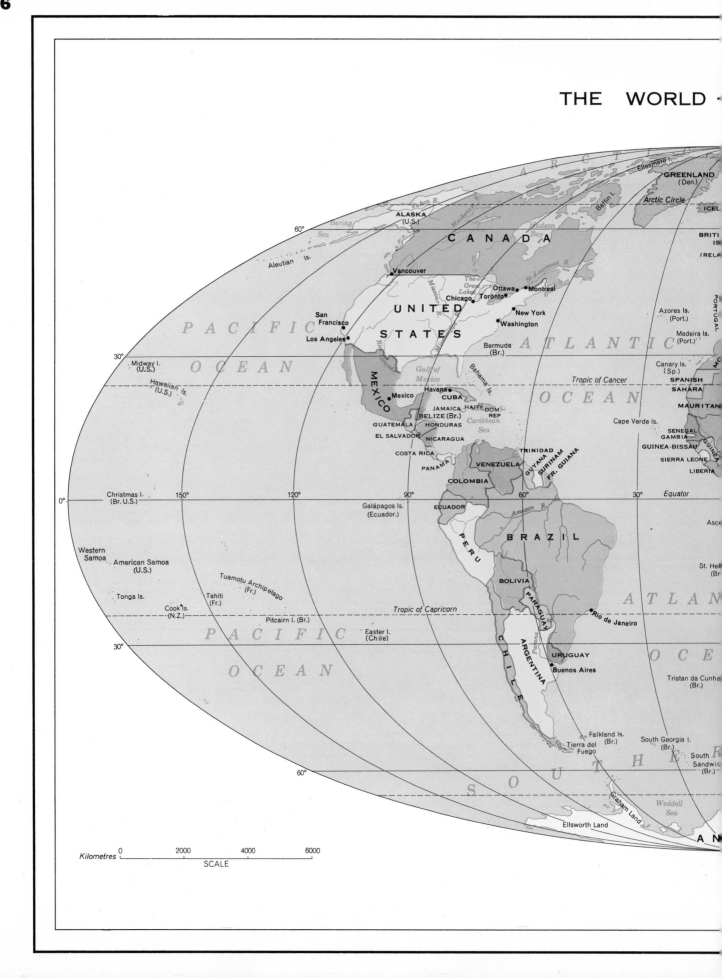

THE   WORLD

GREENLAND
(Den.)

Arctic Circle

ICEL

Ellesmere I.

Baffin I.

ALASKA
(U.S.)

Yukon R.

Bering
Sea

60°

C A N A D A

Hudson
Bay

BRITI
IS

IRELA

Aleutian Is.

Vancouver

The
Great
Lakes

St. Lawrence R.

Ottawa   Montreal

Toronto

Chicago

Azores Is.
(Port.)

PORTUGAL

San
Francisco

U N I T E D

New York

Washington

A T L A N T I C

Madeira Is.
(Port.)

MO

PACIFIC

Los Angeles

S T A T E S

Rio Grande

30°

Missouri R.

Mississippi R.

Bermuda
(Br.)

Canary Is.
(Sp.)

SPANISH

O C E A N

Midway I.
(U.S.)

Gulf of
Mexico

Bahama Is.

Tropic of Cancer

O C E A N

SAHARA

Hawaiian Is.
(U.S.)

MEXICO

Mexico

Havana

CUBA

JAMAICA   HAITI
BELIZE (Br.)   DOM
REP

MAURITAN

Cape Verde Is.

GUATEMALA

HONDURAS

Caribbean
Sea

SENEGAL
GAMBIA

EL SALVADOR   NICARAGUA

GUINEA-BISSAU

GUINE

COSTA RICA

TRINIDAD

SIERRA LEONE

PANAMA

VENEZUELA

GUYANA

SURINAM

FR. GUIANA

LIBERIA

COLOMBIA

0°

Christmas I.
(Br. U.S.)

150°

120°

90°

60°

30°

Equator

Galápagos Is.
(Ecuador.)

ECUADOR

Amazon R.

Asce

PERU

B R A Z I L

Western
Samoa

American Samoa
(U.S.)

BOLIVIA

St. Hel
(Br

PARAGUAY

A T L A N

Tonga Is.

Tuamotu Archipelago
(Fr.)

Tropic of Capricorn

Rio de Janeiro

Tahiti
(Fr.)

Cook Is.
(N.Z.)

Pitcairn I. (Br.)

Paraná R.

URUGUAY

O C E

30°

Easter I.
(Chile)

CHILE

ARGENTINA

Buenos Aires

PACIFIC

Tristan da Cunha
(Br.)

O C E A N

Falkland Is.
(Br.)

South Georgia I.
(Br.)

Tierra del
Fuego

South R

South
Sandwic
(Br.)

60°

S O U T H E

Graham Land

Weddell
Sea

Ellsworth Land

A N

Kilometres   0   2000   4000   6000

SCALE

POLITICAL DIVISIONS

THE WORLD

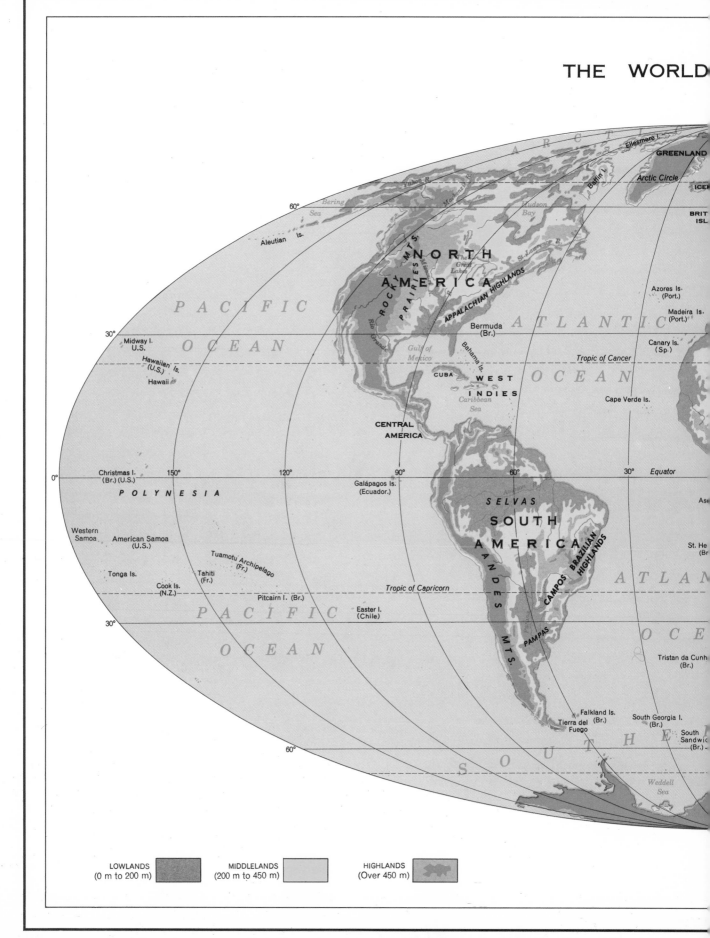

ANDFORMS – RELIEF

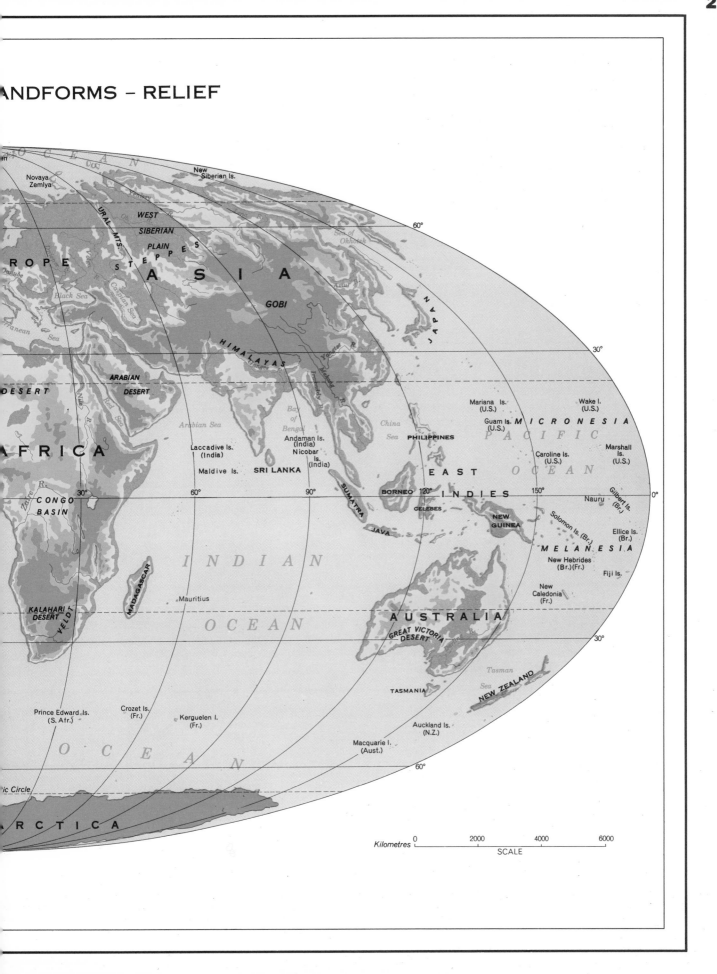

LANDFORMS – RELIEF

Novaya
Zemlya

New
Siberian Is.

URAL MTS.

WEST
SIBERIAN
PLAIN

STEPPES

ROPE

ASIA

GOBI

Sea of
Okhotsk

60°

HIMALAYAS

Ganges

Yangtze R.

Mekong R.

JAPAN

30°

ARABIAN
DESERT

DESERT

Red Sea

Arabian Sea

Bay
of
Bengal

China
Sea

Mariana Is.
(U.S.)

Wake I.
(U.S.)

AFRICA

Laccadive Is.
(India)

Andaman Is.
(India)
Nicobar
Is.
(India)

Guam Is.
(U.S.)

MICRONESIA

PACIFIC

Maldive Is.

SRI LANKA

PHILIPPINES

Caroline Is.
(U.S.)

Marshall
Is.
(U.S.)

CONGO
BASIN

30°

60°

90°

120°

SUMATRA

Borneo

EAST

INDIES

150°

OCEAN

Nauru

Gilbert Is.
(Br.)

0°

Zaire R.

CELEBES

JAVA

NEW
GUINEA

Solomon Is. (Br.)

Ellice Is.
(Br.)

MELANESIA

INDIAN

New Hebrides
(Br.)(Fr.)

Fiji Is.

MADAGASCAR

Mauritius

New
Caledonia
(Fr.)

KALAHARI
DESERT

VELDT

OCEAN

AUSTRALIA

GREAT VICTORIA
DESERT

30°

TASMANIA

Tasman
Sea

NEW ZEALAND

Prince Edward Is.
(S. Afr.)

Crozet Is.
(Fr.)

Kerguelen I.
(Fr.)

Auckland Is.
(N.Z.)

OCEAN

Macquarie I.
(Aust.)

60°

ic Circle

ARCTICA

Kilometres 0   2000   4000   6000

SCALE

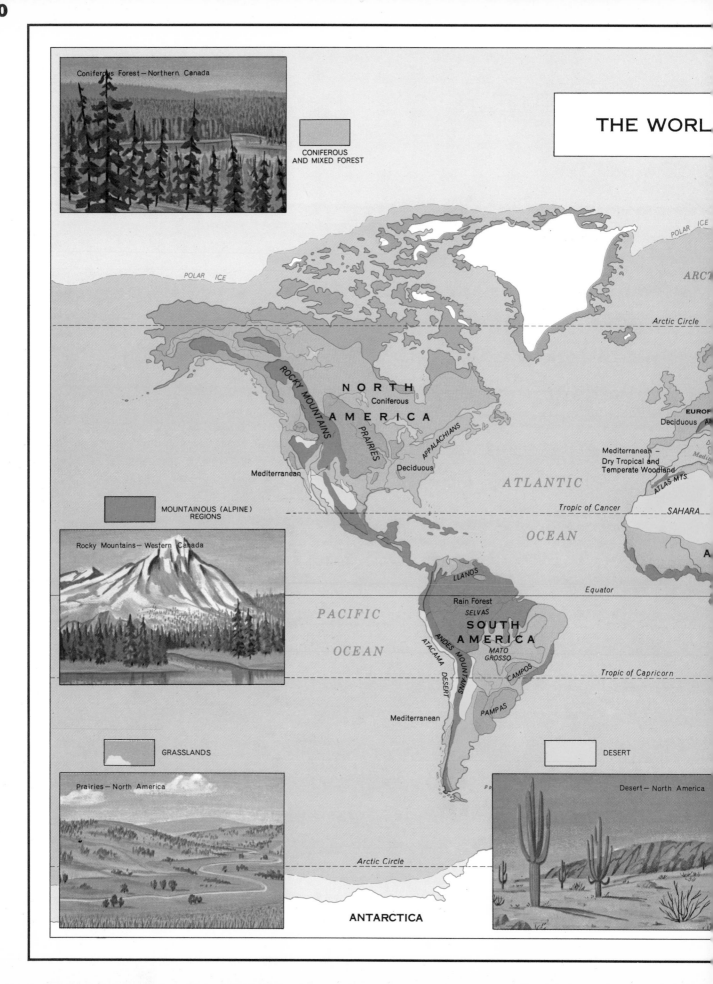

THE WORL

Coniferous Forest — Northern Canada

CONIFEROUS
AND MIXED FOREST

MOUNTAINOUS (ALPINE)
REGIONS

Rocky Mountains — Western Canada

GRASSLANDS

Prairies — North America

DESERT

Desert — North America

POLAR ICE

Arctic Circle

NORTH
AMERICA

Coniferous

PRAIRIES

ROCKY MOUNTAINS

APPALACHIANS

Mediterranean

Deciduous

ATLANTIC

OCEAN

Tropic of Cancer

EUROP
Deciduous

Mediterranean —
Dry Tropical and
Temperate Woodland

ATLAS MTS.

SAHARA

PACIFIC

OCEAN

LLANOS

Rain Forest
SELVAS

SOUTH
AMERICA

ATACAMA DESERT

ANDES MOUNTAINS

MATO
GROSSO

CAMPOS

Tropic of Capricorn

Mediterranean

PAMPAS

Equator

POLAR ICE

ARC

Arctic Circle

ANTARCTICA

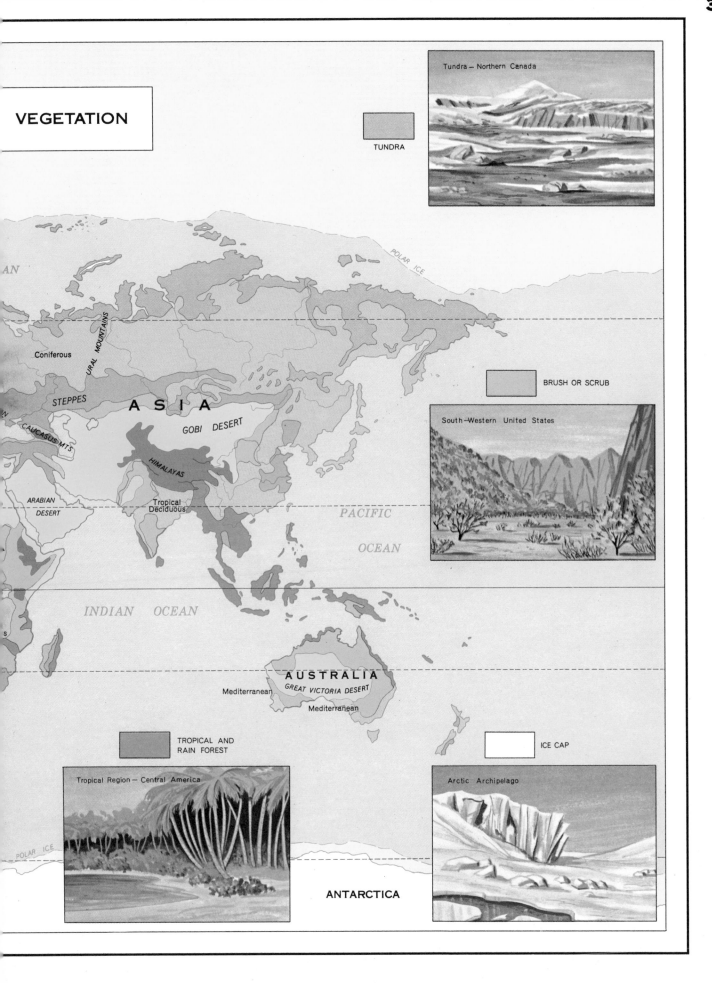

VEGETATION

Tundra — Northern Canada

TUNDRA

BRUSH OR SCRUB

South-Western United States

POLAR ICE

AN

Coniferous

URAL MOUNTAINS

STEPPES

A S I A

GOBI DESERT

CAUCASUS MTS.

HIMALAYAS

ARABIAN DESERT

Tropical Deciduous

PACIFIC

OCEAN

INDIAN OCEAN

AUSTRALIA

GREAT VICTORIA DESERT

Mediterranean

Mediterranean

TROPICAL AND RAIN FOREST

ICE CAP

Tropical Region — Central America

Arctic Archipelago

POLAR ICE

ANTARCTICA

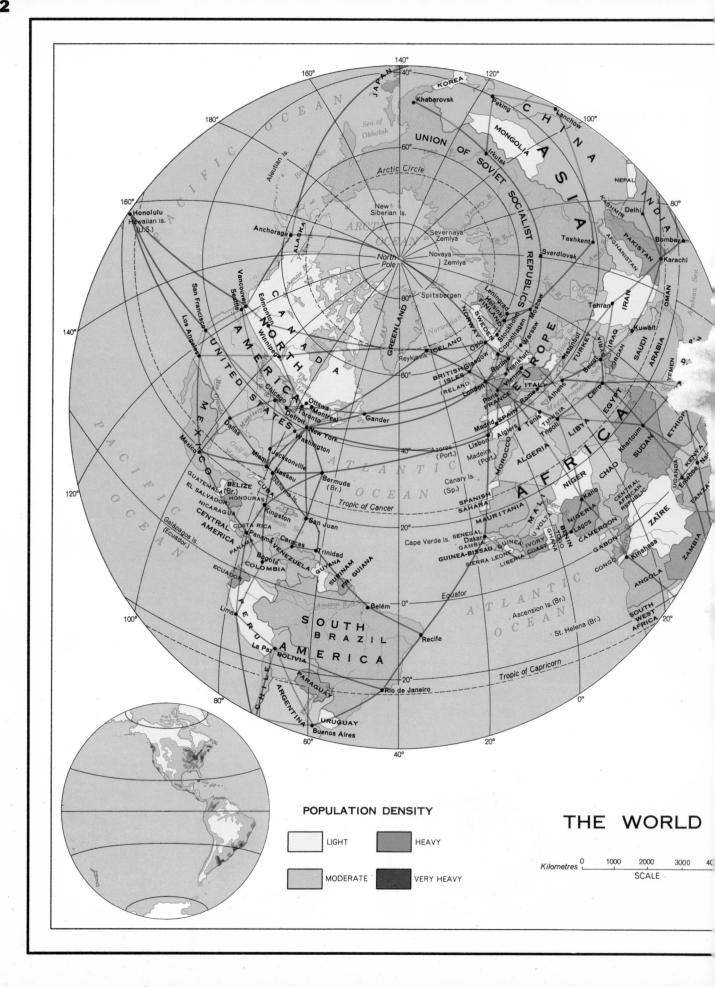

POPULATION DENSITY

LIGHT

HEAVY

MODERATE

VERY HEAVY

THE WORLD

Kilometres 0   1000   2000   3000   40

SCALE

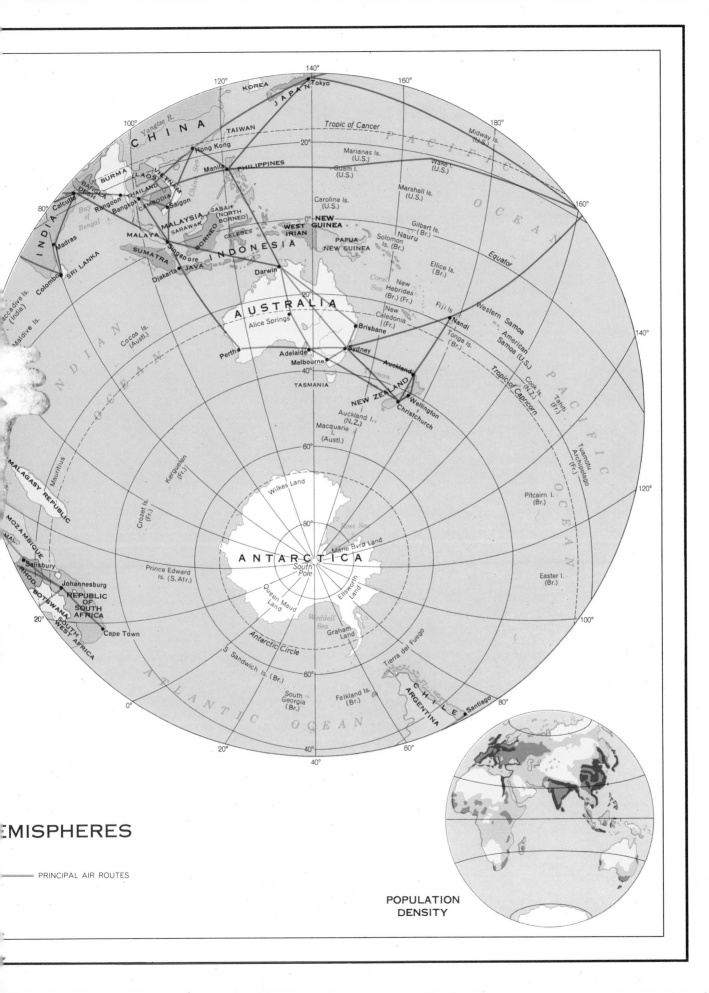

EMISPHERES

— PRINCIPAL AIR ROUTES

POPULATION DENSITY

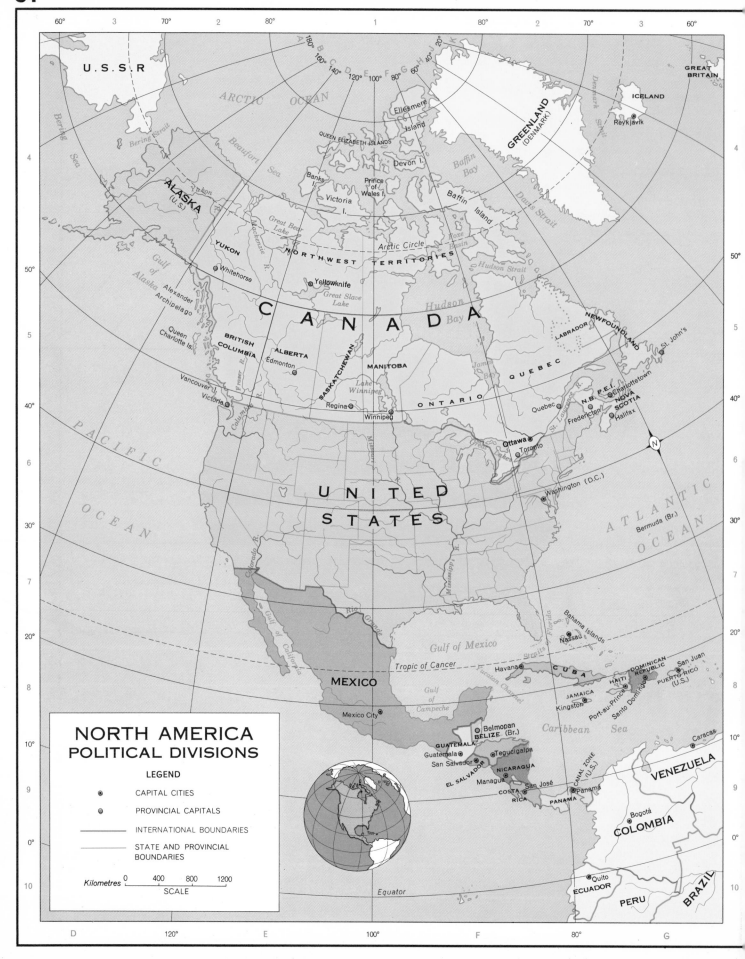

NORTH AMERICA
POLITICAL DIVISIONS

LEGEND

◉ CAPITAL CITIES

● PROVINCIAL CAPITALS

—— INTERNATIONAL BOUNDARIES

—— STATE AND PROVINCIAL BOUNDARIES

Kilometres 0 400 800 1200
SCALE

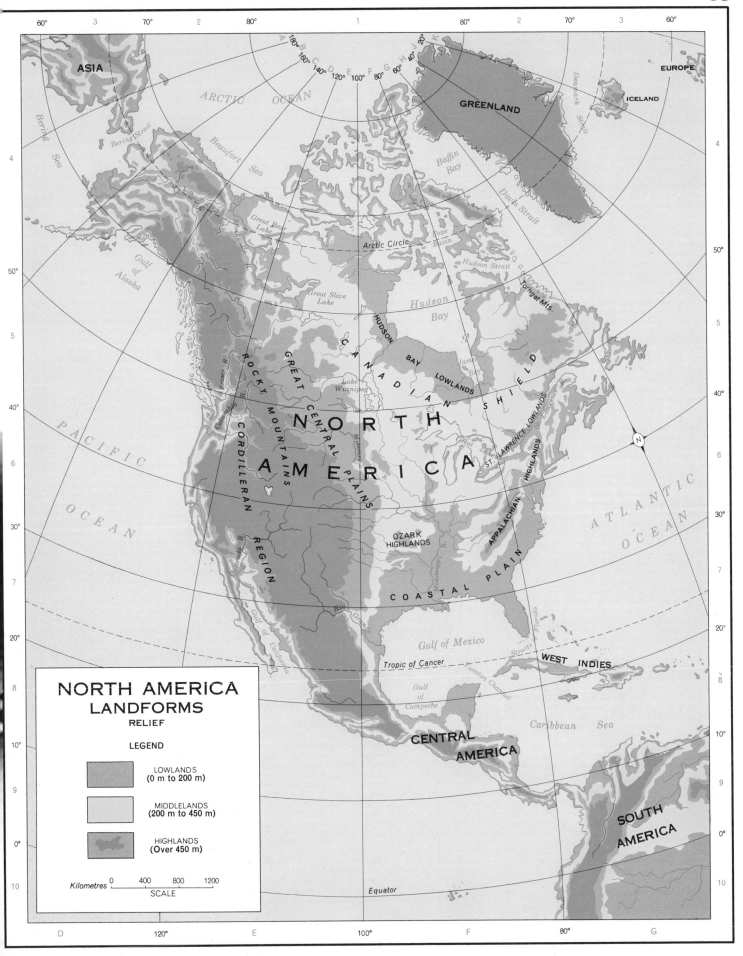

ASIA

ARCTIC OCEAN

Bering Strait

Bering Sea

Beaufort Sea

GREENLAND

EUROPE

ICELAND

Denmark Strait

Baffin Bay

Davis Strait

Gulf of Alaska

Great Bear Lake

Arctic Circle

Foxe Basin

Hudson Strait

Torngat Mts.

Great Slave Lake

Hudson Bay

James Bay

BAY LOWLANDS

CANADIAN SHIELD

PACIFIC OCEAN

ROCKY MOUNTAINS

CORDILLERAN REGION

GREAT CENTRAL PLAINS

Lake Winnipeg

NORTH AMERICA

Fraser R.

Columbia R.

Missouri R.

St. Lawrence Lowlands

St. Lawrence

Great

HIGHLANDS

APPALACHIAN

ATLANTIC OCEAN

N

OZARK HIGHLANDS

Mississippi R.

Colorado R.

Rio Grande

COASTAL PLAIN

Florida

Straits of Florida

WEST INDIES

Gulf of California

Gulf of Mexico

Tropic of Cancer

Gulf of Campeche

Yucatan Channel

Caribbean Sea

CENTRAL AMERICA

SOUTH AMERICA

Equator

NORTH AMERICA
LANDFORMS
RELIEF

LEGEND

LOWLANDS
(0 m to 200 m)

MIDDLELANDS
(200 m to 450 m)

HIGHLANDS
(Over 450 m)

Kilometres 0   400   800   1200
SCALE

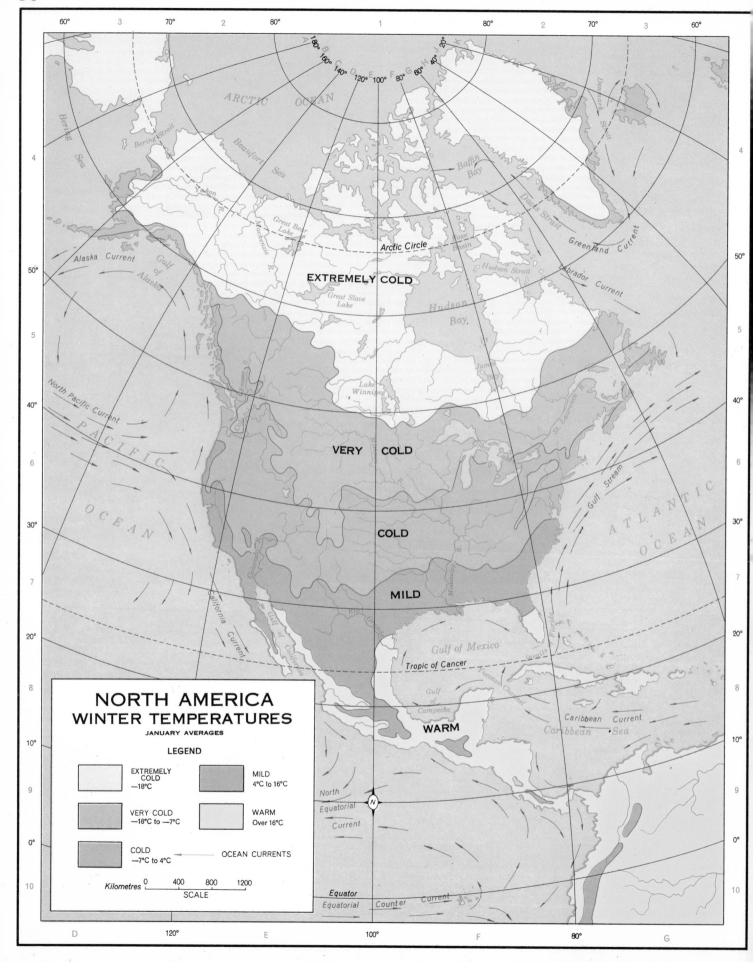

NORTH AMERICA
WINTER TEMPERATURES
JANUARY AVERAGES

LEGEND

EXTREMELY COLD	—18°C	MILD	4°C to 16°C
VERY COLD	—18°C to —7°C	WARM	Over 16°C
COLD	—7°C to 4°C	→	OCEAN CURRENTS

Kilometres 0 400 800 1200
SCALE

EXTREMELY COLD

VERY COLD

COLD

MILD

WARM

ARCTIC OCEAN

PACIFIC OCEAN

ATLANTIC OCEAN

Bering Strait
Beaufort Sea
Baffin Bay
Denmark Strait
Davis Strait
Greenland Current
Labrador Current
Alaska Current
Gulf of Alaska
Arctic Circle
Foxe Basin
Hudson Strait
Great Bear Lake
Mackenzie R.
Great Slave Lake
Hudson Bay
James Bay
Lake Winnipeg
North Pacific Current
St. Lawrence R.
Great Lakes
Gulf Stream
Mississippi R.
California Current
Colorado R.
Gulf of California
Rio Grande
Tropic of Cancer
Gulf of Mexico
Strait of Florida
Yucatan Channel
Gulf of Campeche
Caribbean Current
Caribbean Sea
North Equatorial Current
Equator
Equatorial Counter Current

N

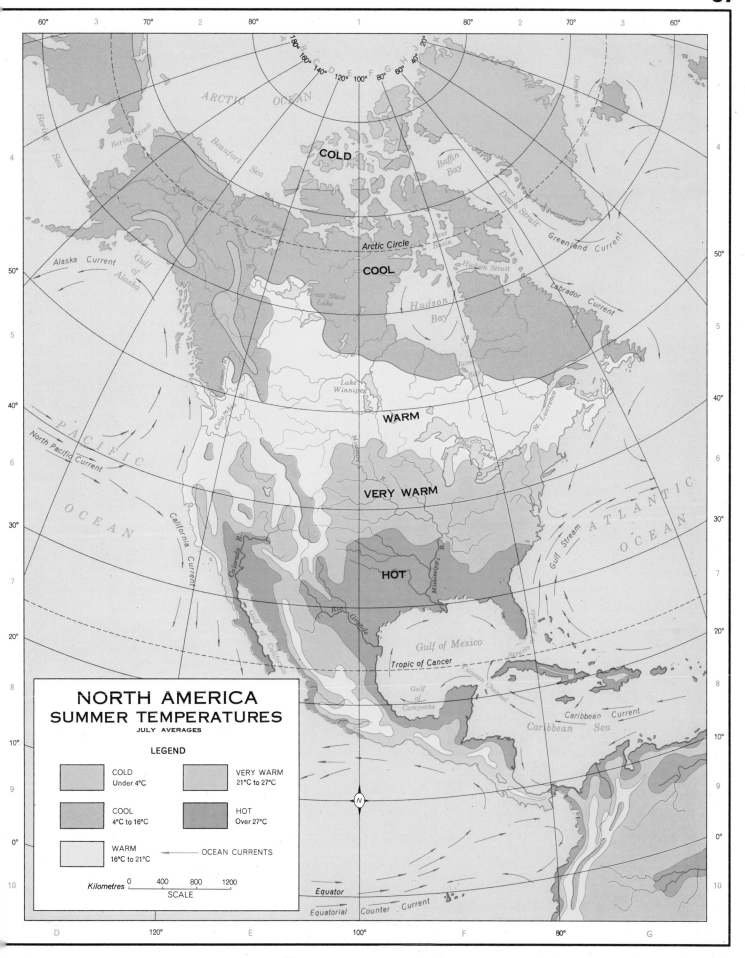

ARCTIC OCEAN

Bering Sea

Beaufort Sea

Bering Strait

COLD

Baffin Bay

Denmark Strait

Davis Strait

Greenland Current

Arctic Circle

COOL

Foxe Basin

Hudson Strait

Alaska Current

Gulf of Alaska

Great Bear Lake

Labrador Current

Great Slave Lake

Hudson Bay

Yukon R.

Mackenzie R.

PACIFIC

North Pacific Current

Lake Winnipeg

James Bay

St. Lawrence

WARM

OCEAN

Fraser R.

Columbia R.

Missouri R.

Great Lakes

ATLANTIC

VERY WARM

Gulf Stream

OCEAN

California Current

Colorado R.

Mississippi R.

HOT

Rio Grande

Florida

Gulf of California

Tropic of Cancer

Straits of Florida

Gulf of Mexico

Yucatan Channel

Gulf of Campeche

Caribbean Current

Caribbean Sea

N

Equator

Equatorial Counter Current

NORTH AMERICA
SUMMER TEMPERATURES
JULY AVERAGES

LEGEND

COLD
Under 4°C

VERY WARM
21°C to 27°C

COOL
4°C to 16°C

HOT
Over 27°C

WARM
16°C to 21°C

OCEAN CURRENTS

Kilometres   0   400   800   1200
SCALE

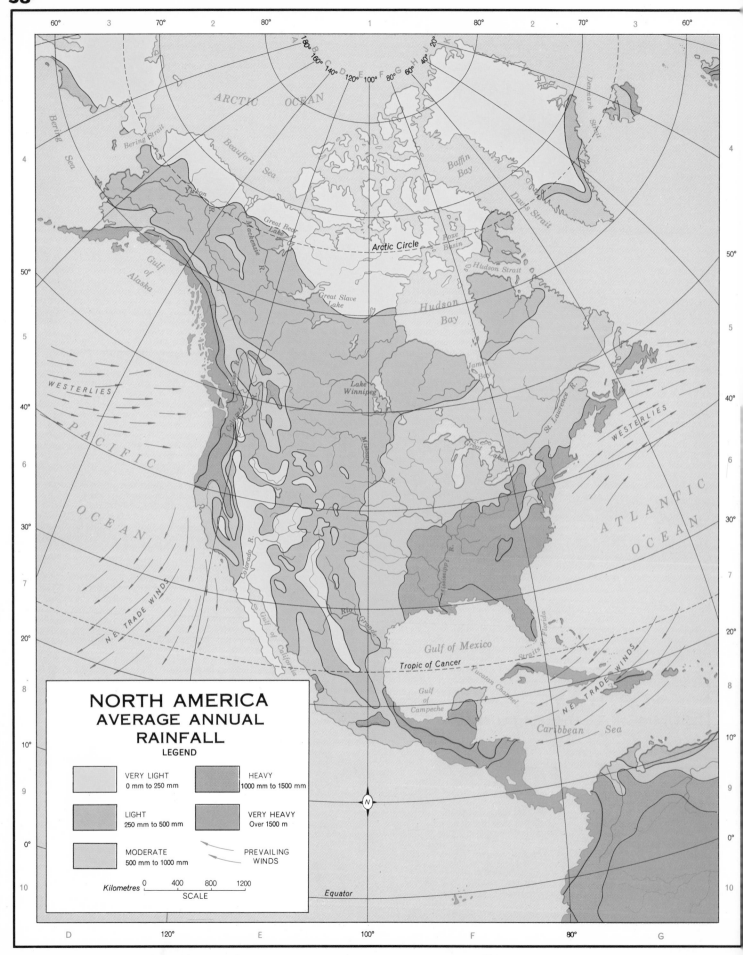

NORTH AMERICA
AVERAGE ANNUAL
RAINFALL
LEGEND

VERY LIGHT 0 mm to 250 mm		HEAVY 1000 mm to 1500 mm	
LIGHT 250 mm to 500 mm		VERY HEAVY Over 1500 m	
MODERATE 500 mm to 1000 mm		PREVAILING WINDS	

Kilometres 0   400   800   1200
SCALE

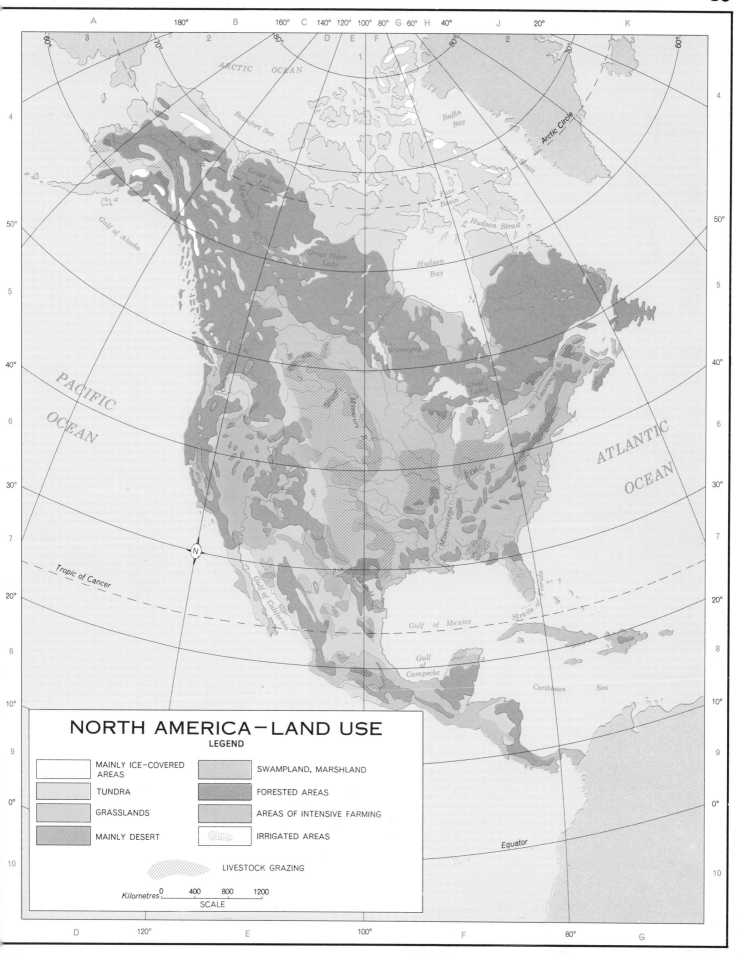

NORTH AMERICA—LAND USE

LEGEND

☐	MAINLY ICE-COVERED AREAS		SWAMPLAND, MARSHLAND
☐	TUNDRA		FORESTED AREAS
☐	GRASSLANDS		AREAS OF INTENSIVE FARMING
☐	MAINLY DESERT		IRRIGATED AREAS
			LIVESTOCK GRAZING

Kilometres 0   400   800   1200
SCALE

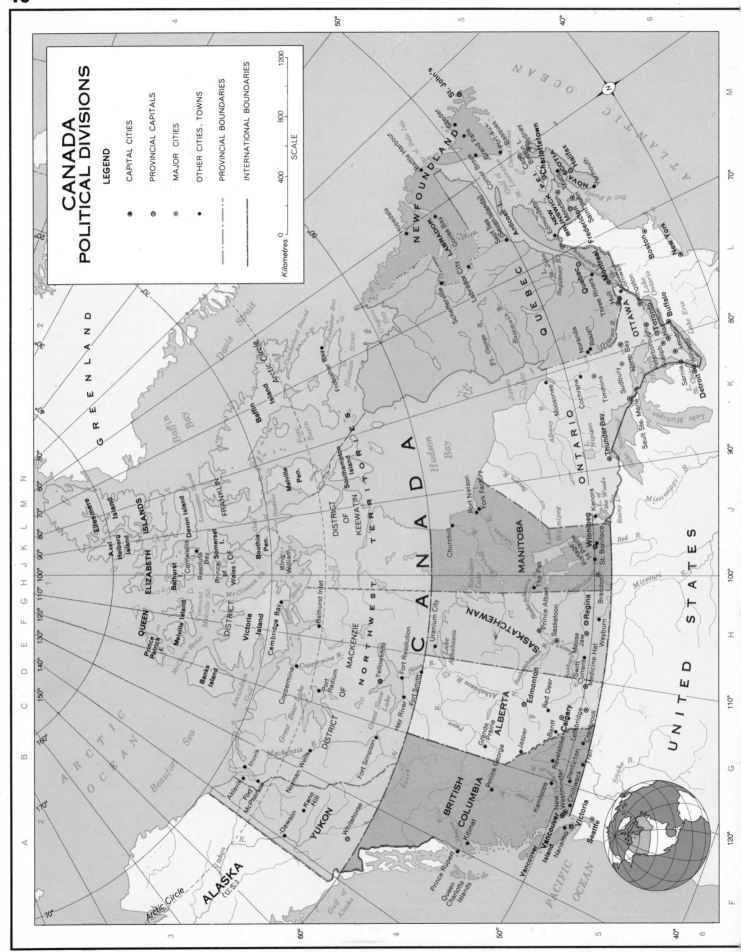

CANADA
POLITICAL DIVISIONS

LEGEND

⊙	CAPITAL CITIES
◉	PROVINCIAL CAPITALS
⊙	MAJOR CITIES
•	OTHER CITIES, TOWNS
—·—·—	PROVINCIAL BOUNDARIES
———	INTERNATIONAL BOUNDARIES

SCALE

Kilometres 0 400 800 1200

GREENLAND

ATLANTIC OCEAN

N

ARCTIC OCEAN

Beaufort Sea

ALASKA (U.S.)

Arctic Circle

Davis Strait

Baffin Bay

Baffin Island

QUEEN ELIZABETH ISLANDS

Ellesmere Island

Axel Heiberg Island

Devon Island

Prince Patrick I.

Melville Island

Banks Island

Victoria Island

Prince of Wales I.

Boothia Pen.

Melville Pen.

Southampton Island

FRANKLIN

DISTRICT OF KEEWATIN

NORTHWEST TERRITORIES

DISTRICT OF MACKENZIE

Hudson Bay

Foxe Basin

Hudson Strait

Ungava Bay

NEWFOUNDLAND

LABRADOR

St. John's

Gander

Corner Brook

Hopedale

QUEBEC

ONTARIO

MANITOBA

SASKATCHEWAN

ALBERTA

BRITISH COLUMBIA

YUKON

Whitehorse

Dawson

Keno Hill

Inuvik

Aklavik

Fort McPherson

Norman Wells

Fort Simpson

Yellowknife

Hay River

Fort Resolution

Fort Smith

Uranium City

Lake Athabasca

Great Bear Lake

Great Slave Lake

Coppermine

Port Radium

Cambridge Bay

Bathurst Inlet

Resolute

Churchill

Port Nelson

York Factory

The Pas

Prince Albert

Saskatoon

Edmonton

Red Deer

Calgary

Lethbridge

Medicine Hat

Swift Current

Moose Jaw

Regina

Weyburn

Brandon

Winnipeg

St. Boniface

Kenora

Thunder Bay

Sault Ste. Marie

Sudbury

Timmins

Cochrane

Moosonee

OTTAWA

Toronto

Hamilton

London

Windsor

Detroit

Buffalo

New York

Boston

Montreal

Quebec

Three Rivers

Hull

Kingston

Peterborough

Guelph

Sarnia

Noranda

Rouyn

Schefferville

Labrador City

Sept Iles

Gaspé

Fredericton

Saint John

Moncton

Halifax

Charlottetown

NEW BRUNSWICK

NOVA SCOTIA

P.E.I.

Bay of Fundy

Gulf of St. Lawrence

PACIFIC OCEAN

Victoria

Vancouver

Vancouver Island

Nanaimo

New Westminster

Chilliwack

Kamloops

Penticton

Trail

Revelstoke

Prince George

Prince Rupert

Kitimat

Queen Charlotte Islands

Banff

Jasper

Grande Prairie

Gulf of Alaska

Seattle

UNITED STATES

CANADA

Arctic Circle

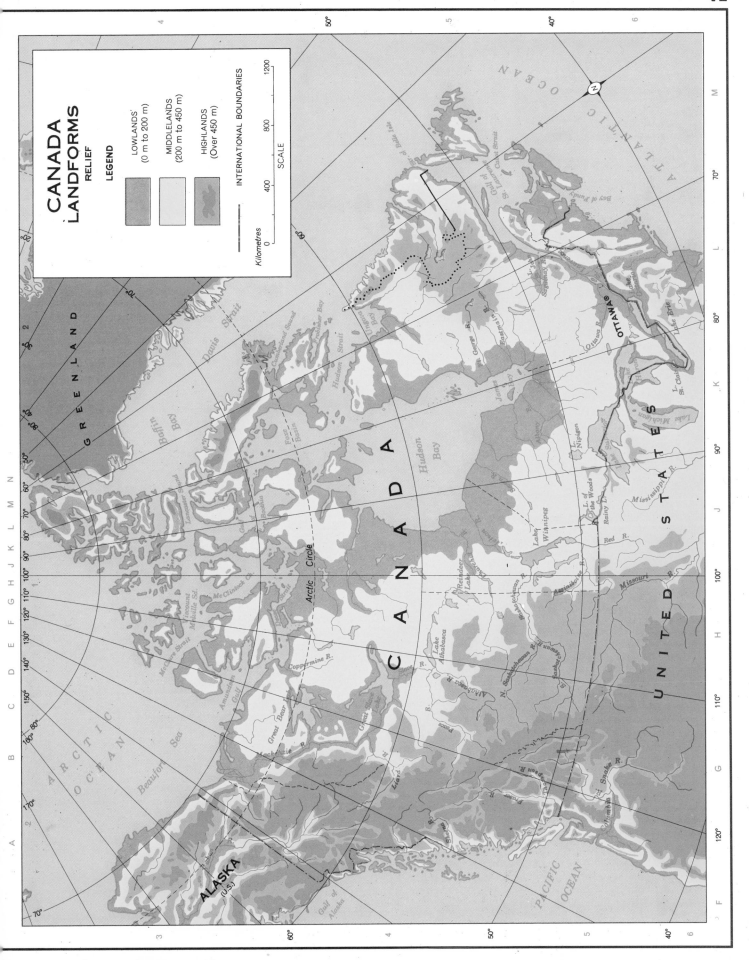

CANADA LANDFORMS

RELIEF

LEGEND

LOWLANDS
(0 m to 200 m)

MIDDLELANDS
(200 m to 450 m)

HIGHLANDS
(Over 450 m)

INTERNATIONAL BOUNDARIES

SCALE

1200

800

400

0

Kilometres

GREENLAND

ATLANTIC OCEAN

ARCTIC OCEAN

PACIFIC OCEAN

Beaufort Sea

Baffin Bay

Davis Strait

Hudson Bay

Hudson Strait

Foxe Basin

Cumberland Sound

Frobisher Bay

Ungava Bay

Gulf of Boothia

Lancaster Sound

M'Clintock Ch.

McClure Strait

Melville Sd.

Viscount Melville Sd.

Amundsen Gulf

Coppermine R.

Great Bear Lake

Great Slave Lake

Mackenzie R.

Liard R.

Peace R.

Athabasca R.

Lake Athabasca

Churchill R.

Fraser R.

Columbia R.

Snake R.

Arctic Circle

CANADA

UNITED STATES

ALASKA
(U.S.)

Gulf of Alaska

Lake Winnipeg

Lake Winnipegosis

L. Manitoba

Reindeer Lake

N. Saskatchewan R.

S. Saskatchewan R.

Saskatchewan R.

Nelson R.

Assiniboine R.

Red R.

Rainy L.

L. of the Woods

L. Nipigon

Lake Superior

Lake Huron

Lake Michigan

Lake Erie

L. St. Clair

Georgian Bay

Missouri R.

Mississippi R.

Albany R.

Moose R.

Attawapiskat R.

Severn R.

James Bay

Eastmain R.

La Grande R.

Koksoak R.

OTTAWA

Ottawa R.

St. Lawrence R.

Lake Ontario

L. St. Jean

Saguenay R.

Gulf of St. Lawrence

St. Lawrence

Cabot Strait

Bay of Fundy

Strait of Belle Isle

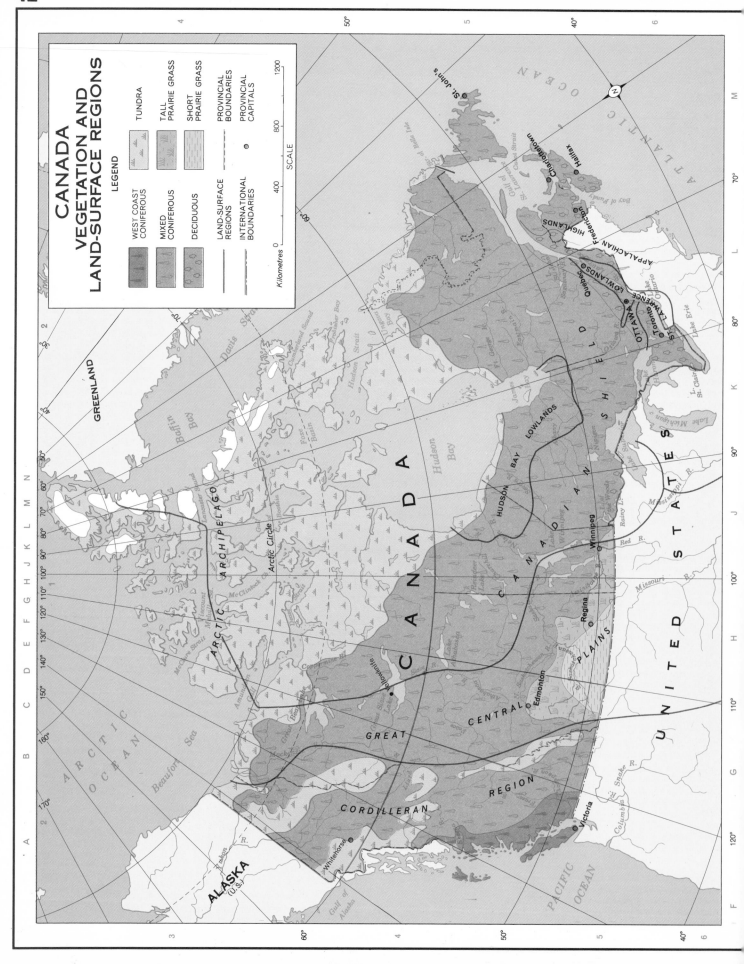

CANADA
VEGETATION AND
LAND-SURFACE REGIONS

LEGEND

WEST COAST CONIFEROUS

MIXED CONIFEROUS

DECIDUOUS

LAND-SURFACE REGIONS

INTERNATIONAL BOUNDARIES

TUNDRA

TALL PRAIRIE GRASS

SHORT PRAIRIE GRASS

PROVINCIAL BOUNDARIES

PROVINCIAL CAPITALS

SCALE

Kilometres

0   400   800   1200

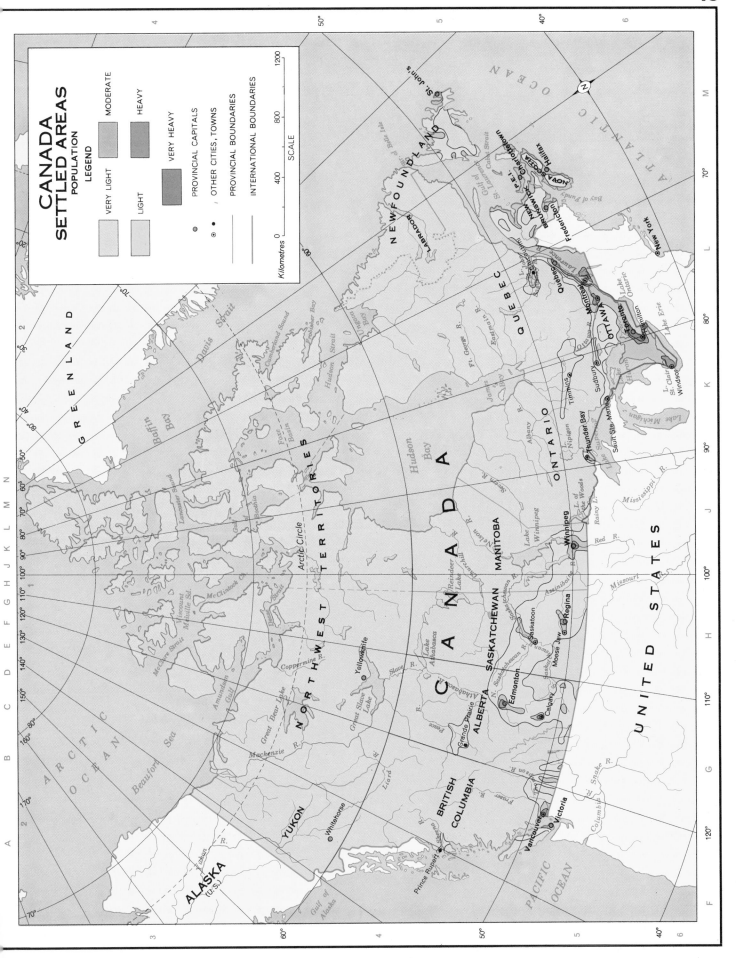

CANADA
SETTLED AREAS
POPULATION
LEGEND

VERY LIGHT   MODERATE

LIGHT   HEAVY

VERY HEAVY

⊙ PROVINCIAL CAPITALS

⊙, • OTHER CITIES, TOWNS

PROVINCIAL BOUNDARIES

INTERNATIONAL BOUNDARIES

SCALE

Kilometres 0   400   800   1200

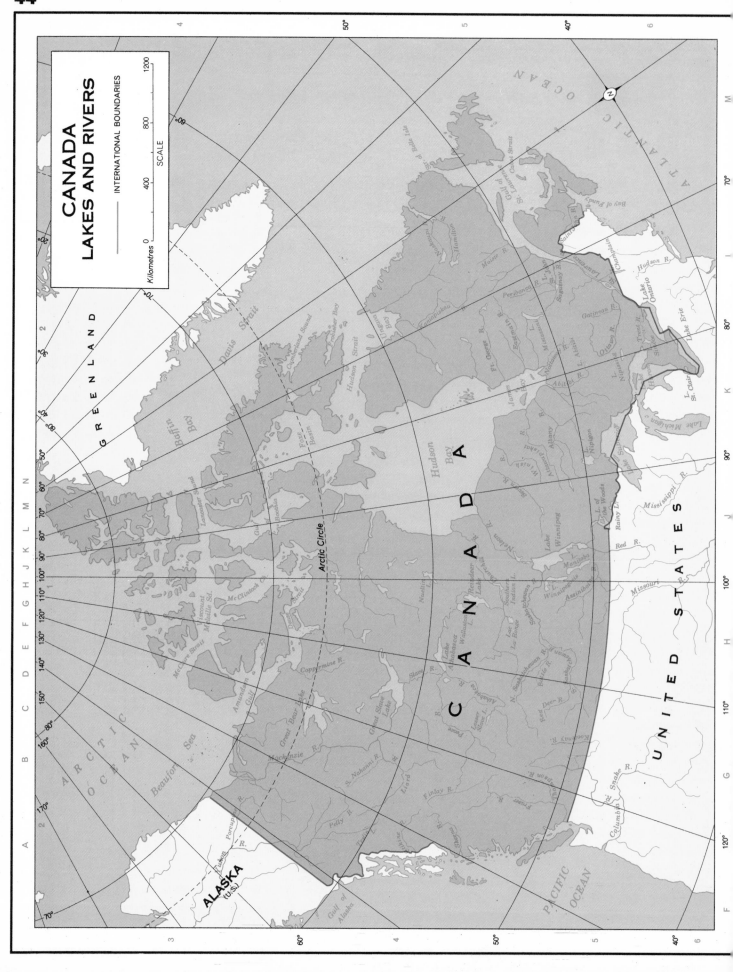

CANADA
LAKES AND RIVERS

——— INTERNATIONAL BOUNDARIES

SCALE

Kilometres 0   400   800   1200

GREENLAND

ATLANTIC OCEAN

Gulf of Boothia Isle

St. Lawrence Gulf

Bay of Fundy

Hudson R.

Lake Ontario

L. Erie

L. St. Clair

Lake Michigan

Lake Huron

Lake Superior

Nipigon

L. Nipissing

Ottawa R.

Trent R.

Gatineau R.

St. Lawrence R.

Saguenay R.

L. St. John

Eastmain R.

Moine R.

Hamilton

Périhonca R.

Ft. George R.

Kaniapiskau

Abitibi R.

James Bay

Albany R.

Attawapiskat

Winisk R.

Severn R.

L. of the Woods

Rainy L.

Red R.

Mississippi

Missouri

L. Winnipeg

L. Manitoba

L. Winnipegosis

Assiniboine

N. Saskatchewan R.

S. Saskatchewan R.

Lac la Ronge

Southern Indian L.

Reindeer L.

Churchill R.

Nelson R.

Nuptin R.

Baffin Bay

Davis Strait

Cumberland Sound

Frobisher Bay

Hudson Strait

Ungava Bay

Hudson Bay

Fox Basin

Lancaster Sound

Boothia

Gulf of Boothia

Bellot Strait

McClintock

Viscount Melville Sd.

McClure Strait

Amundsen Gulf

Coppermine R.

Dease Strait

Great Bear Lake

Great Slave Lake

Slave R.

Athabasca

Lake Athabasca

Wollaston L.

Peace R.

Lesser Slave L.

Arctic Circle

ARCTIC OCEAN

Beaufort Sea

Mackenzie R.

Liard R.

S. Nahanni R.

Finlay R.

Pelly R.

Porcupine R.

Yukon R.

Stikine R.

Fraser R.

Skeena R.

Peace R.

Red Deer R.

Bow R.

Saskatchewan R.

Kootenay R.

Columbia R.

Snake R.

Missouri

C A N A D A

U N I T E D   S T A T E S

ALASKA
(U.S.)

Gulf of Alaska

PACIFIC OCEAN

80° 70° 60° 50° 40° 30°

70° 80° 90° 100° 110° 120° 130° 140° 150° 160° 170° 80° 70°

A B C D E F G H J K L M N

2 3 4 5 6

40° 50° 40° 60°

120° 110° 100° 90° 80° 70°

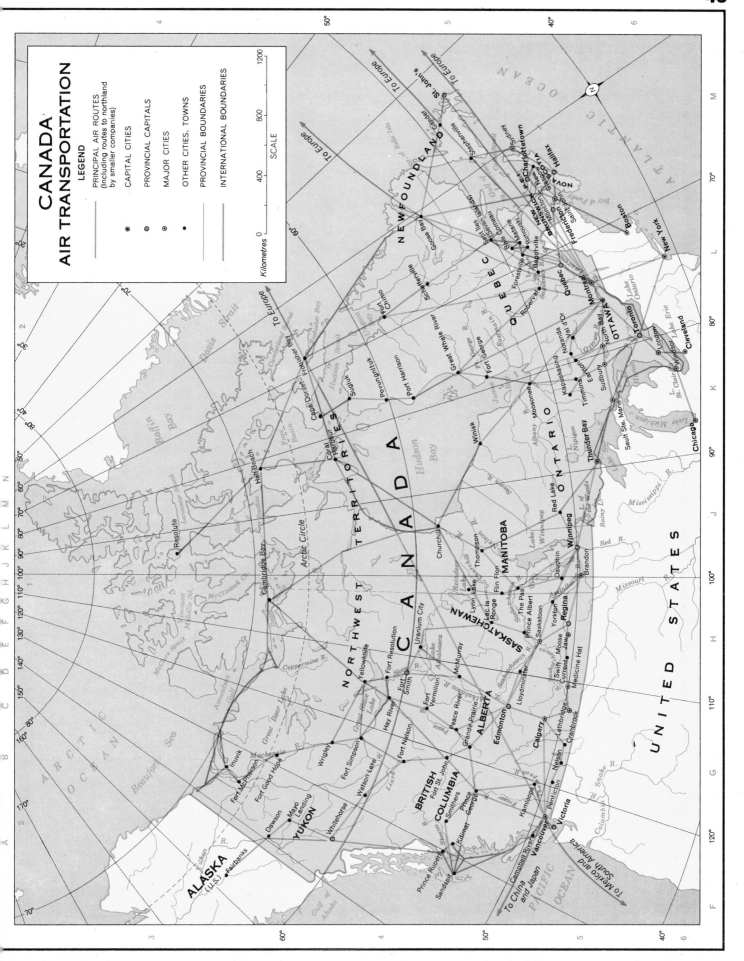

CANADA
AIR TRANSPORTATION

LEGEND

PRINCIPAL AIR ROUTES
(Including routes to northland
by smaller companies)

⊙ CAPITAL CITIES

⊙ PROVINCIAL CAPITALS

⊙ MAJOR CITIES

• OTHER CITIES, TOWNS

PROVINCIAL BOUNDARIES

INTERNATIONAL BOUNDARIES

SCALE

Kilometres

0   400   800   1200

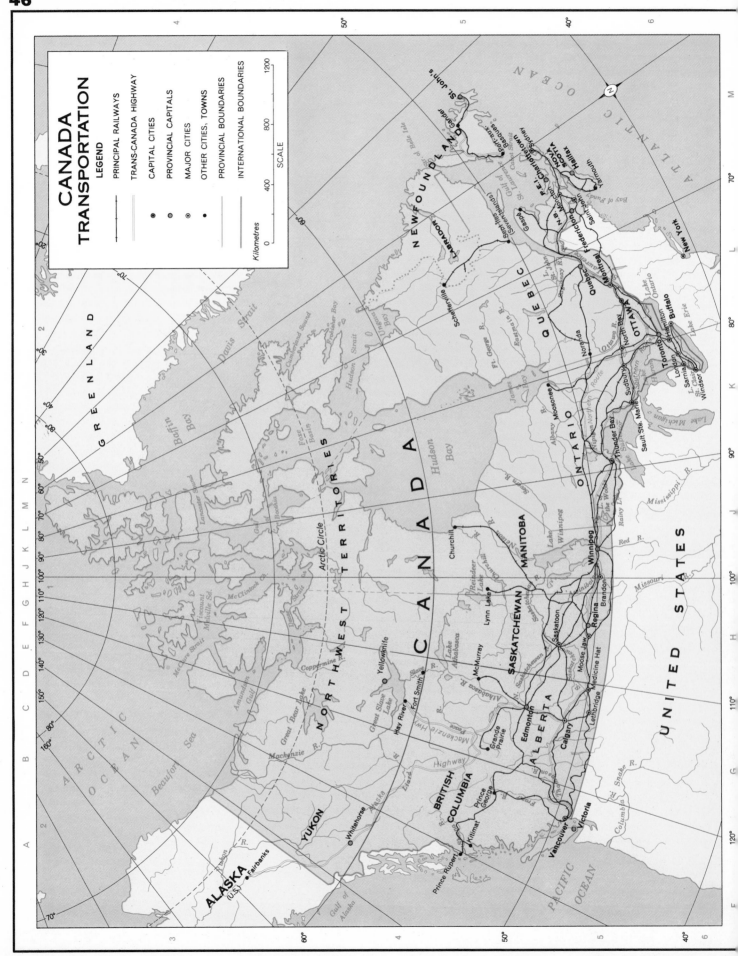

46

CANADA
TRANSPORTATION

LEGEND

PRINCIPAL RAILWAYS
TRANS-CANADA HIGHWAY
CAPITAL CITIES
PROVINCIAL CAPITALS
MAJOR CITIES
OTHER CITIES, TOWNS
PROVINCIAL BOUNDARIES
INTERNATIONAL BOUNDARIES

SCALE

Kilometres

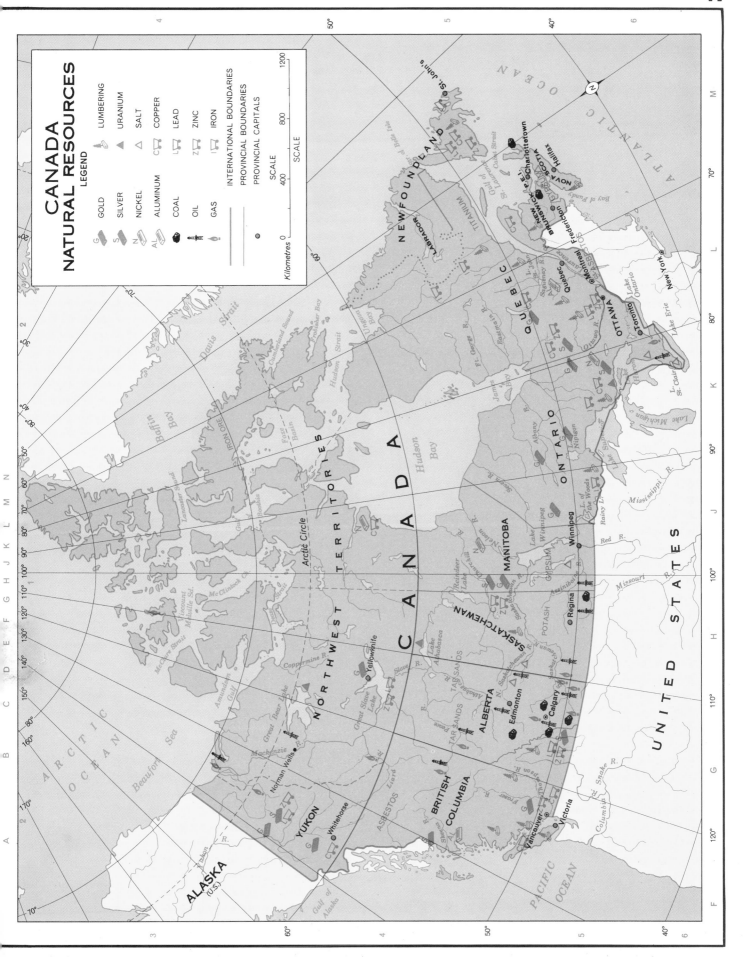

47

CANADA
NATURAL RESOURCES

LEGEND

G GOLD   LUMBERING
S SILVER   URANIUM
N NICKEL   SALT
AL ALUMINUM   COPPER
COAL   LEAD
OIL   ZINC
GAS   IRON

INTERNATIONAL BOUNDARIES
PROVINCIAL BOUNDARIES
PROVINCIAL CAPITALS

SCALE

Kilometres 0   400   800   1200

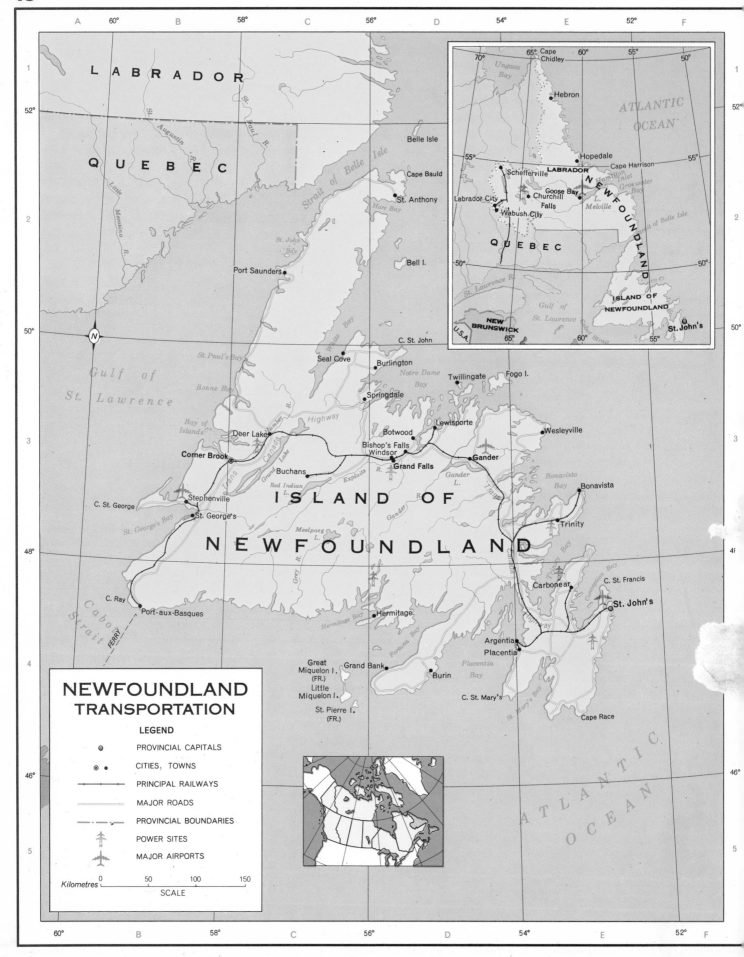

NEWFOUNDLAND
TRANSPORTATION

LEGEND

⊙ PROVINCIAL CAPITALS

⊙ • CITIES, TOWNS

╼╀╼ PRINCIPAL RAILWAYS

═══ MAJOR ROADS

─·─·─ PROVINCIAL BOUNDARIES

POWER SITES

MAJOR AIRPORTS

Kilometres
0   50   100   150
SCALE

Map labels

LABRADOR

QUEBEC

Little Mecatina R.

St. Augustin R.

St. Paul R.

Strait of Belle Isle

Belle Isle

Cape Bauld

St. Anthony

Hare Bay

St. John Bay

Bell I.

Port Saunders

St. Paul's Bay

Gulf of St. Lawrence

Bonne Bay

Bay of Islands

C. St. John

Seal Cove

Burlington

Notre Dame Bay

Twillingate

Fogo I.

Springdale

Highway

Humber R.

Deer Lake

Corner Brook

Botwood

Lewisporte

Wesleyville

Buchans

Grand Lake

Canada

Trans

Bishop's Falls
Windsor

Grand Falls

Exploits R.

Gander

Red Indian L.

ISLAND OF

Stephenville

C. St. George

St. George's

St. George's Bay

Meelpaeg L.

NEWFOUNDLAND

Gander L.

Gander R.

Bonavista Bay

Bonavista

Trinity

Grey R.

Trans

Trinity Bay

Carbonear

C. St. Francis

C. Ray

Port-aux-Basques

Cabot Strait

FERRY

Hermitage Bay

Hermitage

Fortune Bay

Great
Miquelon I.
(FR.)
Little
Miquelon I.

St. Pierre I.
(FR.)

Grand Bank

Burin

C. St. Mary's

Placentia Bay

Argentia
Placentia

Highway

Placentia Bay

St. Mary's Bay

St. John's

Cape Race

ATLANTIC OCEAN

Inset map (Labrador)

Cape Chidley

Ungava Bay

Hebron

ATLANTIC OCEAN

Hopedale

Cape Harrison

LABRADOR

Schefferville

Goose Bay

Churchill Falls

Hamilton Inlet

Groswater Bay

Labrador City

NEWFOUNDLAND

L. Melville

Wabush City

QUEBEC

Strait of Belle Isle

St. Lawrence R.

NEW BRUNSWICK

U.S.A.

Gulf of St. Lawrence

ISLAND OF NEWFOUNDLAND

St. John's

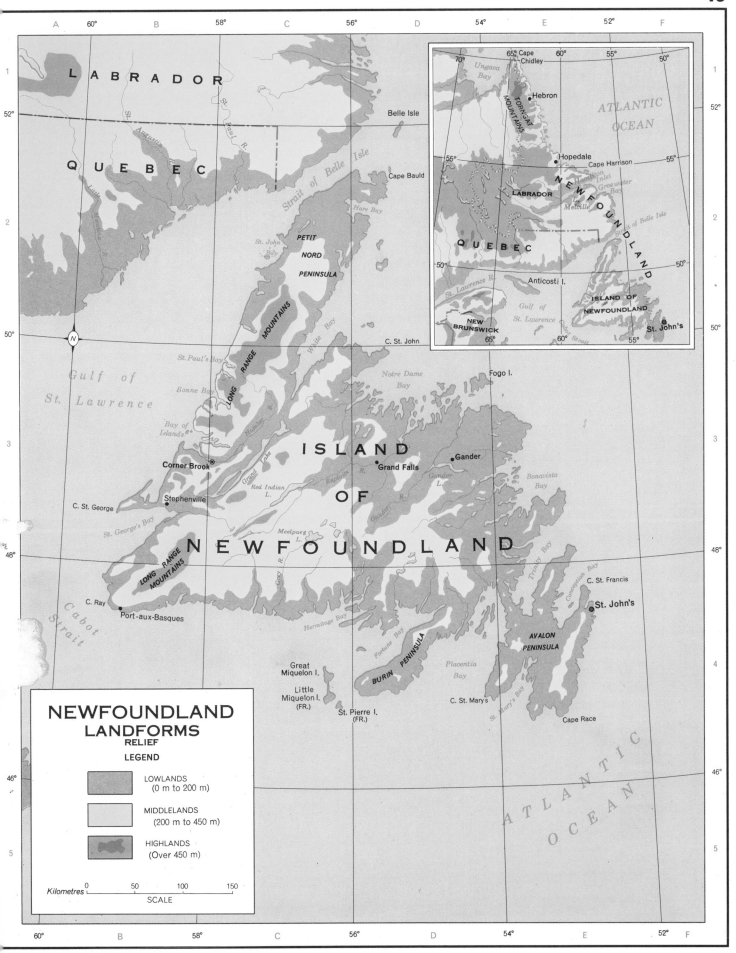

Inset map labels:

65° Cape Chidley
Ungava Bay
Hebron
Torngat Mountains
ATLANTIC OCEAN
Hopedale
Cape Harrison
Hamilton Inlet
Groswater Bay
LABRADOR
Melville
NEWFOUNDLAND
QUEBEC
Strait of Belle Isle
St. Lawrence R.
Anticosti I.
Gulf of St. Lawrence
ISLAND OF NEWFOUNDLAND
NEW BRUNSWICK
Cabot Strait
St. John's

Main map labels:

L A B R A D O R
52°
St. Augustin R.
St. Paul R.
Little Mecatina R.
Q U E B E C
Belle Isle
Cape Bauld
Strait of Belle Isle
Hare Bay
PETIT NORD PENINSULA
St. John Bay
White Bay
LONG RANGE MOUNTAINS
C. St. John
50°
St. Paul's Bay
Notre Dame Bay
Fogo I.
Bonne Bay
Gulf of St. Lawrence
Bay of Islands
Humber R.
ISLAND
Grand Lake
Gander
Corner Brook
Grand Falls
Gander L.
Bonavista Bay
Red Indian L.
Exploits R.
OF
Stephenville
C. St. George
Gander R.
St. George's Bay
Meelpaeg L.
NEWFOUNDLAND
48°
Grey R.
LONG RANGE MOUNTAINS
Trinity Bay
C. St. Francis
Conception Bay
C. Ray
Hermitage Bay
St. John's
Port-aux-Basques
Cabot Strait
Fortune Bay
BURIN PENINSULA
Placentia Bay
AVALON PENINSULA
Great Miquelon I.
Little Miquelon I. (FR.)
St. Pierre I. (FR.)
C. St. Marys
St. Mary's Bay
Cape Race
46°
A T L A N T I C   O C E A N

NEWFOUNDLAND
LANDFORMS
RELIEF
LEGEND

LOWLANDS
(0 m to 200 m)

MIDDLELANDS
(200 m to 450 m)

HIGHLANDS
(Over 450 m)

Kilometres
0   50   100   150
SCALE

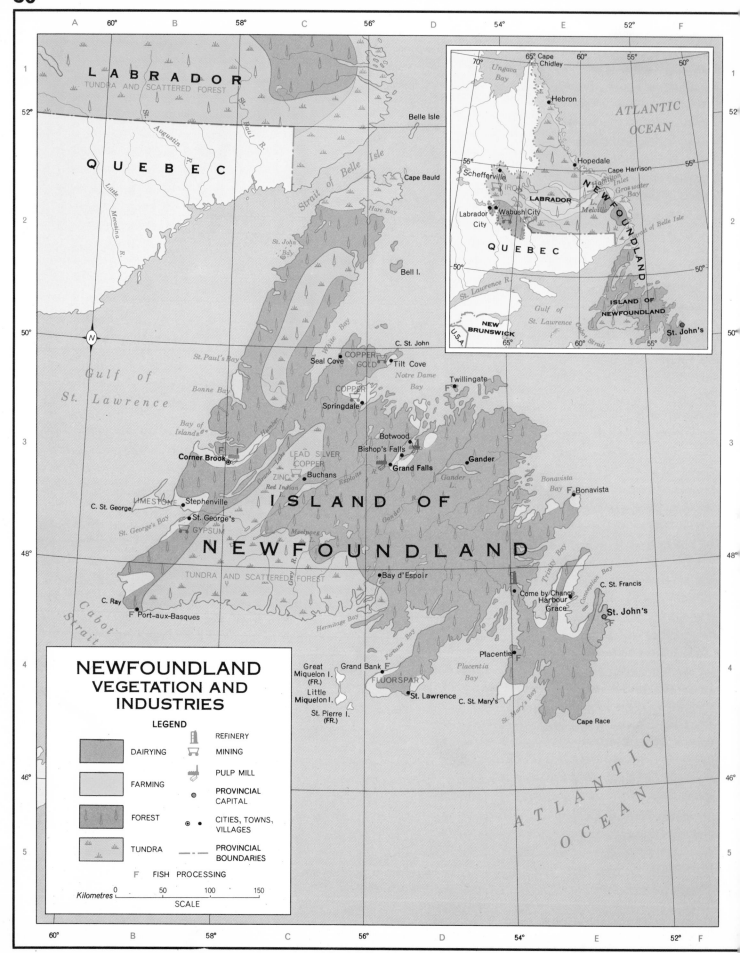

NEWFOUNDLAND
VEGETATION AND INDUSTRIES

LEGEND

DAIRYING

FARMING

FOREST

TUNDRA

REFINERY

MINING

PULP MILL

PROVINCIAL CAPITAL

CITIES, TOWNS, VILLAGES

PROVINCIAL BOUNDARIES

F   FISH PROCESSING

Kilometres   0   50   100   150
SCALE

Map labels

LABRADOR
TUNDRA AND SCATTERED FOREST

QUEBEC

St. Augustin R.

St. Paul R.

Little Mecatina R.

Belle Isle

Strait of Belle Isle

Cape Bauld

Hare Bay

St. John Bay

Bell I.

Gulf of St. Lawrence

White Bay

St. Paul's Bay

Seal Cove

COPPER
GOLD

C. St. John

Tilt Cove

Notre Dame Bay

Twillingate

Bonne Bay

COPPER

Springdale

Bay of Islands

Humber R.

Botwood

Bishop's Falls

Grand Falls

Gander

Corner Brook

Grand Lake

LEAD SILVER COPPER

Buchans

ZINC

Red Indian L.

Exploits R.

Gander L.

Gander R.

Bonavista Bay

Bonavista

C. St. George

LIMESTONE

Stephenville

St. George's

St. George's Bay

GYPSUM

Meelpaeg L.

ISLAND OF

NEWFOUNDLAND

TUNDRA AND SCATTERED FOREST

Bay d'Espoir

Come by Chance

Harbour Grace

C. St. Francis

C. Ray

Port-aux-Basques

Cabot Strait

Hermitage Bay

Great Miquelon I. (FR.)

Grand Bank

Fortune Bay

FLUORSPAR

Little Miquelon I.

St. Pierre I. (FR.)

St. Lawrence

C. St. Mary's

Placentia

Placentia Bay

St. Mary's Bay

Conception Bay

Trinity Bay

St. John's

Cape Race

ATLANTIC OCEAN

Inset map

65° Cape Chidley

Ungava Bay

70°

60°

55°

50°

Hebron

ATLANTIC OCEAN

Schefferville

Hopedale

Cape Harrison

55°

IRON

LABRADOR

Hamilton Inlet

Groswater Bay

L. Melville

Labrador City

Wabush City

QUEBEC

NEWFOUNDLAND

50°

St. Lawrence R.

Gulf of St. Lawrence

Cabot Strait

Strait of Belle Isle

NEW BRUNSWICK

ISLAND OF NEWFOUNDLAND

U.S.A.

65°

60°

St. John's

55°

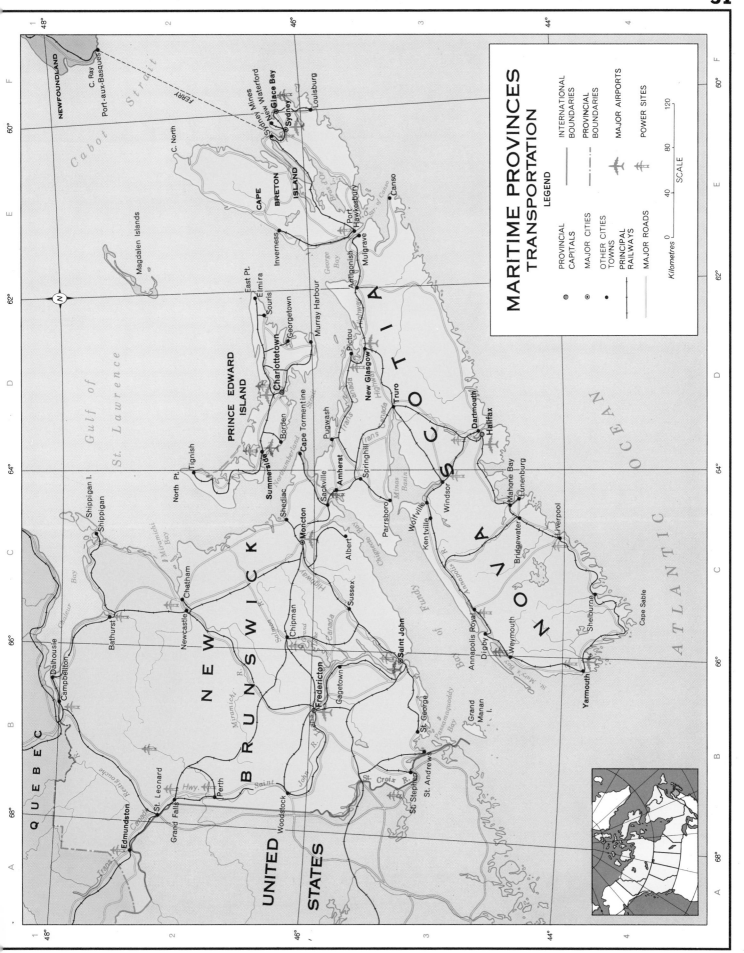

MARITIME PROVINCES
TRANSPORTATION

LEGEND

	INTERNATIONAL BOUNDARIES
PROVINCIAL CAPITALS	PROVINCIAL BOUNDARIES
MAJOR CITIES	MAJOR AIRPORTS
OTHER CITIES TOWNS	POWER SITES
PRINCIPAL RAILWAYS	
MAJOR ROADS	

SCALE

Kilometres 0   40   80   120

NEWFOUNDLAND

C. Ray
Port-aux-Basques

FERRY

Cabot Strait

C. North

Magdalen Islands

Gulf of St. Lawrence

Sydney Mines
New Waterford
Glace Bay
Sydney
Louisburg

CAPE BRETON ISLAND

Inverness

Bras d'Or L.
Str. of Canso

Port Hawkesbury
Mulgrave
Canso

Antigonish

East Pt.
Elmira
Souris

Georgetown
Murray Harbour

George Bay

Pictou
New Glasgow

PRINCE EDWARD ISLAND

Charlottetown

Truro

Summerside
Borden
Cape Tormentine

N O V A   S C O T I A

Dartmouth
Halifax

Tignish
North Pt.

Pugwash

Trans Canada Highway

Windsor
Mahone Bay
Lunenburg

Shediac
Moncton

Amherst
Springhill
Parrsboro

Minas Basin

Wolfville
Kentville

Liverpool

Shippigan I.
Shippigan

Miramichi Bay

Chaleur Bay

Chatham

Sackville

Albert

Sussex

Bay of Fundy

Annapolis Royal
Digby

Bridgewater

Shelburne

Cape Sable

Dalhousie
Campbellton

Bathurst

Newcastle

N E W   B R U N S W I C K

Miramichi R.

Salmon R.

Chipman

Grand Lake

Saint John

St. George
St. Andrews

Passamaquoddy Bay
Grand Manan I.

St. Mary's Bay

Weymouth
Yarmouth

Q U E B E C

Restigouche R.

St. Leonard
Perth

Hwy.

Edmundston
Grand Falls
Woodstock

Trans Canada

Saint John R.

Fredericton
Gagetown

St. Croix R.
St. Stephen

U N I T E D   S T A T E S

A T L A N T I C   O C E A N

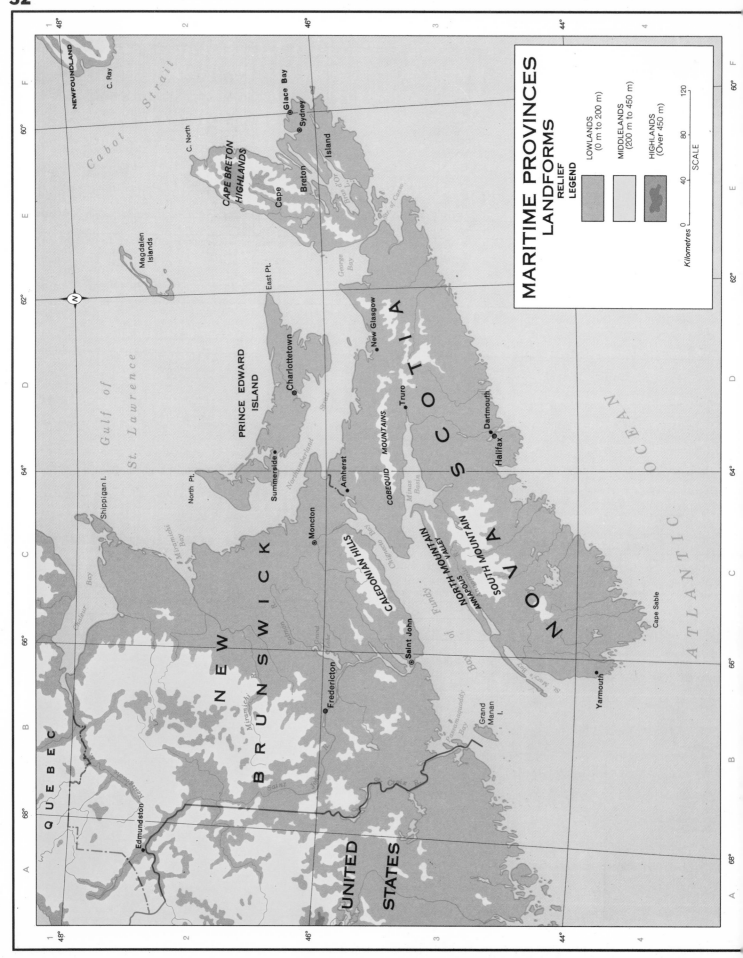

MARITIME PROVINCES
LANDFORMS

RELIEF
LEGEND

LOWLANDS
(0 m to 200 m)

MIDDLELANDS
(200 m to 450 m)

HIGHLANDS
(Over 450 m)

SCALE

Kilometres 0   40   80   120

NEWFOUNDLAND

C. Ray

Cabot   Strait

Gulf of
St. Lawrence

Magdalen
Islands

QUEBEC

NEW BRUNSWICK

UNITED
STATES

Edmundston

Fredericton

Saint John

Moncton

Shippigan I.

Chaleur Bay

Salmon R.

Miramichi Bay

North Pt.

Summerside

Charlottetown

PRINCE EDWARD
ISLAND

Northumberland Strait

East Pt.

C. North

Cape Breton
CAPE BRETON
HIGHLANDS

Cape Breton Island

Bras d'Or Lake

Glace Bay

Sydney

George Bay

Str. of Canso

New Glasgow

Truro

COBEQUID MOUNTAINS

Amherst

Chignecto Bay

Minas Basin

NOVA SCOTIA

NORTH MOUNTAIN
ANNAPOLIS VALLEY

SOUTH MOUNTAIN

Bay of Fundy

CALEDONIAN HILLS

Passamaquoddy Bay

Grand Manan I.

St. Mary's Bay

Yarmouth

Cape Sable

Dartmouth
Halifax

ATLANTIC   OCEAN

N

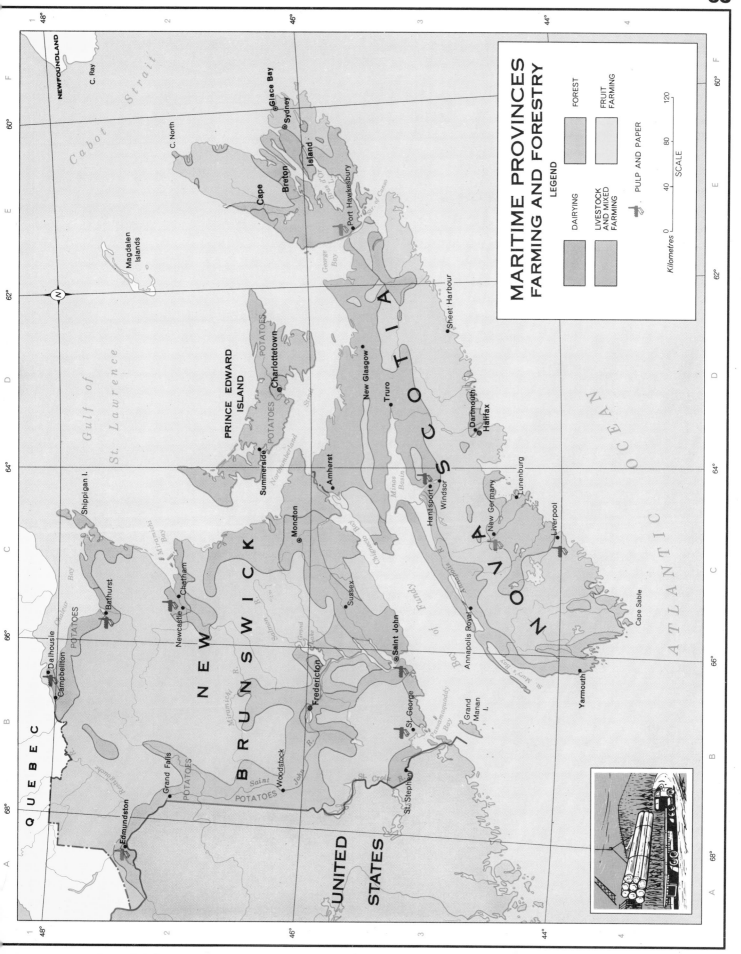

53

MARITIME PROVINCES
FARMING AND FORESTRY

LEGEND

DAIRYING

LIVESTOCK
AND MIXED
FARMING

FOREST

FRUIT
FARMING

PULP AND PAPER

SCALE

Kilometres   0   40   80   120

NEWFOUNDLAND

C. Ray

Cabot   Strait

Glace Bay

Sydney

C. North

Cape   Breton   Island

Bras d'Or L.

Port Hawkesbury

Str. of Canso

Magdalen
Islands

George
Bay

Sheet Harbour

N   S   C   O   T   I   A

PRINCE EDWARD
ISLAND

POTATOES

Charlottetown

POTATOES

Summerside

Northumberland   Str.

Gulf   of   St. Lawrence

New Glasgow

Truro

Dartmouth
Halifax

Amherst

Minas   Basin

Windsor

Hantsport

Lunenburg

New Germany

Liverpool

Shippigan I.

Miramichi
Bay

Bathurst

Chatham

Newcastle

N   E   W   B   R   U   N   S   W   I   C   K

Moncton

Chignecto   Bay

Sussex

Saint John

Cape Sable

ATLANTIC   OCEAN

Chaleur   Bay

Restigouche   R.

Dalhousie

Campbellton

POTATOES

Grand Falls

POTATOES

Edmundston

QUEBEC

Miramichi   R.

Salmon   R.

Grand   Lake

Saint   John   R.

Woodstock

POTATOES

Fredericton

St. George

St. Croix R.

St. Stephen

Passamaquoddy
Bay

Grand Manan
I.

Bay   of   Fundy

Annapolis   R.

Annapolis Royal

St. Mary's Bay

Yarmouth

UNITED
STATES

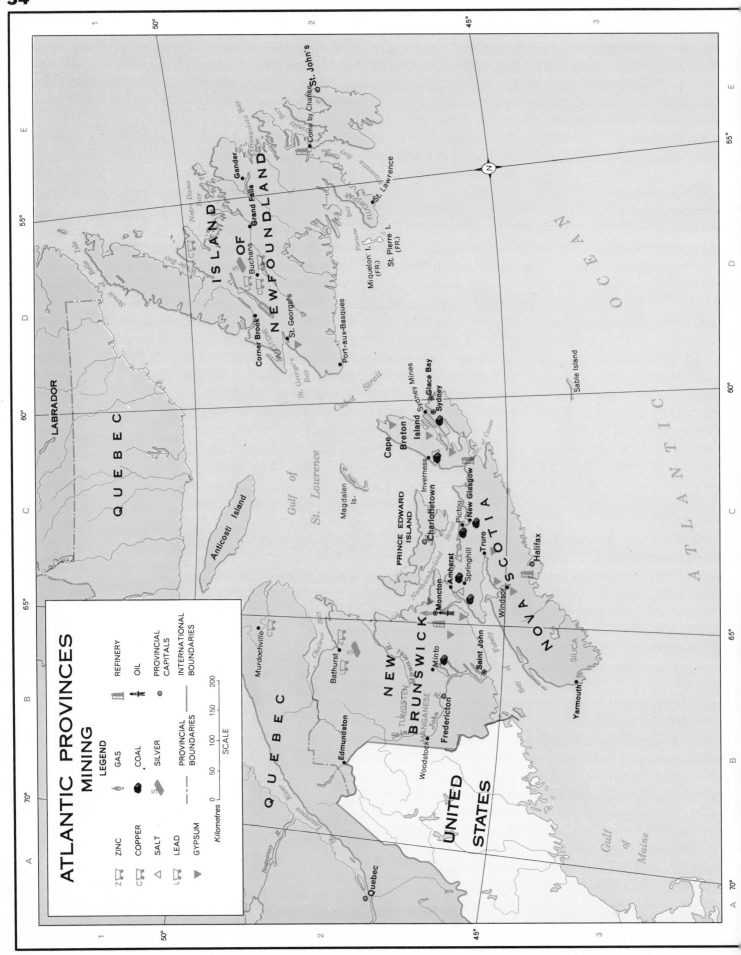

54

ATLANTIC PROVINCES
MINING

LEGEND

Z	ZINC		GAS
C	COPPER	•	COAL
△	SALT	S	SILVER
L	LEAD		REFINERY
▼	GYPSUM		OIL
		●	PROVINCIAL CAPITALS
		—·—·—	INTERNATIONAL BOUNDARIES
		———	PROVINCIAL BOUNDARIES

SCALE

Kilometres

0   50   100   150   200

LABRADOR

QUEBEC

QUEBEC

UNITED STATES

NEW BRUNSWICK

Edmundston

Woodstock

Fredericton

Saint John

Bathurst

Murdochville

Minto

Moncton

TUNGSTEN

MANGANESE

Saint John R.

Miramichi R.

Chaleur Bay

Gulf of Maine

Bay of Fundy

SILICA

Yarmouth

NOVA SCOTIA

Windsor

Halifax

Truro

Amherst

Springhill

New Glasgow

Pictou

Inverness

Charlottetown

PRINCE EDWARD ISLAND

Northumberland Strait

Strait of Canso

Cape Breton Island

Sydney Mines

Glace Bay

Sydney

Magdalen Is.

Gulf of St. Lawrence

Anticosti Island

Cabot Strait

Port-aux-Basques

St. George's

Corner Brook

Buchans

Grand Falls

Gander

Come by Chance

St. John's

NEWFOUNDLAND

ISLAND OF

St. George's Bay

Bonavista Bay

Trinity Bay

Notre Dame Bay

White Bay

Strait of Belle Isle

Belle Isle

Miquelon I. (FR.)

St. Pierre I. (FR.)

Fortune Bay

Placentia Bay

St. Lawrence

FLUORSPAR

Sable Island

ATLANTIC OCEAN

Quebec

St. Lawrence River

Saguenay R.

Lawrence River

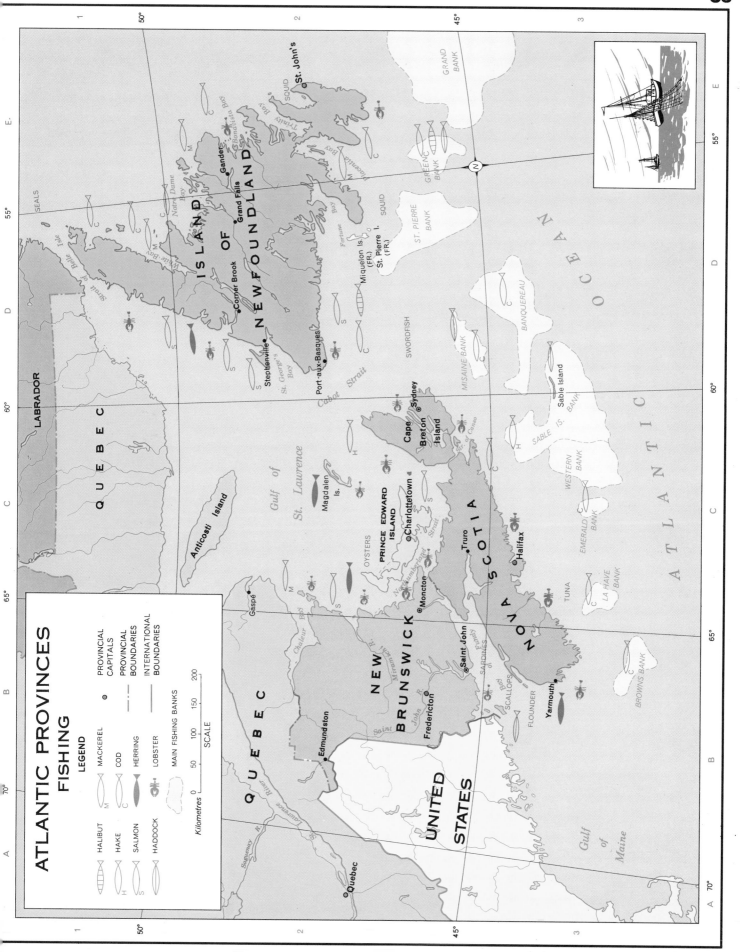

ATLANTIC PROVINCES
FISHING

LEGEND

HALIBUT

HAKE

SALMON

HADDOCK

MACKEREL

COD

HERRING

LOBSTER

● PROVINCIAL CAPITALS

PROVINCIAL BOUNDARIES

INTERNATIONAL BOUNDARIES

MAIN FISHING BANKS

SCALE

Kilometres 0   50   100   150   200

LABRADOR

QUEBEC

ISLAND OF NEWFOUNDLAND

St. John's

Gander

Grand Falls

Corner Brook

Stephenville

Port-aux-Basques

Notre Dame Bay

Bonavista Bay

Trinity Bay

White Bay

Bay

Fortune Bay

St. George's Bay

Cabot Strait

SEALS

Strait of Belle Isle

Belle Isle

Miquelon Is. (FR.)

St. Pierre I. (FR.)

SQUID

ST. PIERRE BANK

GREEN BANK

GRAND BANK

GREEN BANK

SWORDFISH

BANQUEREAU

MISAINE BANK

SABLE IS. BANK

Sable Island

WESTERN BANK

EMERALD BANK

LA HAVE BANK

BROWNS BANK

ATLANTIC OCEAN

ATLANTIC

Gulf of St. Lawrence

Anticosti Island

Magdalen Is.

PRINCE EDWARD ISLAND

Charlottetown

Northumberland Strait

Strait of Canso

Cape Breton Island

Sydney

Truro

Halifax

NOVA SCOTIA

Yarmouth

OYSTERS

SCALLOPS

FLOUNDER

TUNA

SARDINES

NEW BRUNSWICK

Moncton

Saint John

Fredericton

Edmundston

Gaspé

Chaleur Bay

Miramichi R.

Saint John R.

Bay of Fundy

QUEBEC

Quebec

St. Lawrence River

Saguenay R.

Restigouche R.

UNITED STATES

Gulf of Maine

50°

55°

60°

65°

70°

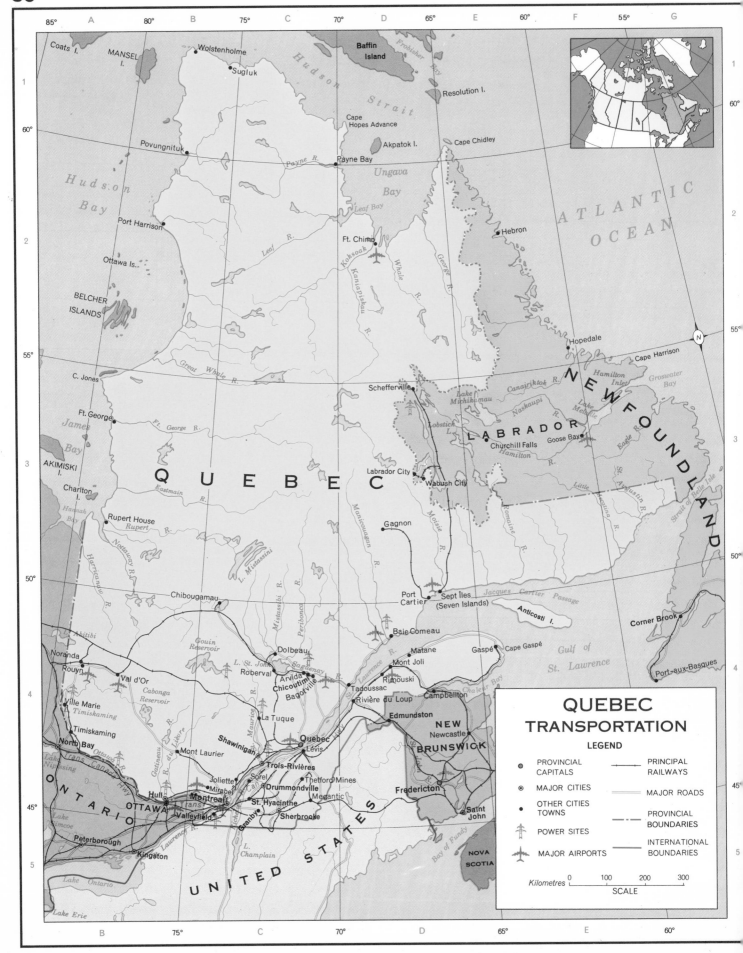

QUEBEC TRANSPORTATION

LEGEND

● PROVINCIAL CAPITALS		┼┼ PRINCIPAL RAILWAYS
◉ MAJOR CITIES		═ MAJOR ROADS
● OTHER CITIES TOWNS		─·─ PROVINCIAL BOUNDARIES
⌁ POWER SITES		─ INTERNATIONAL BOUNDARIES
✈ MAJOR AIRPORTS		

Kilometres 0   100   200   300
SCALE

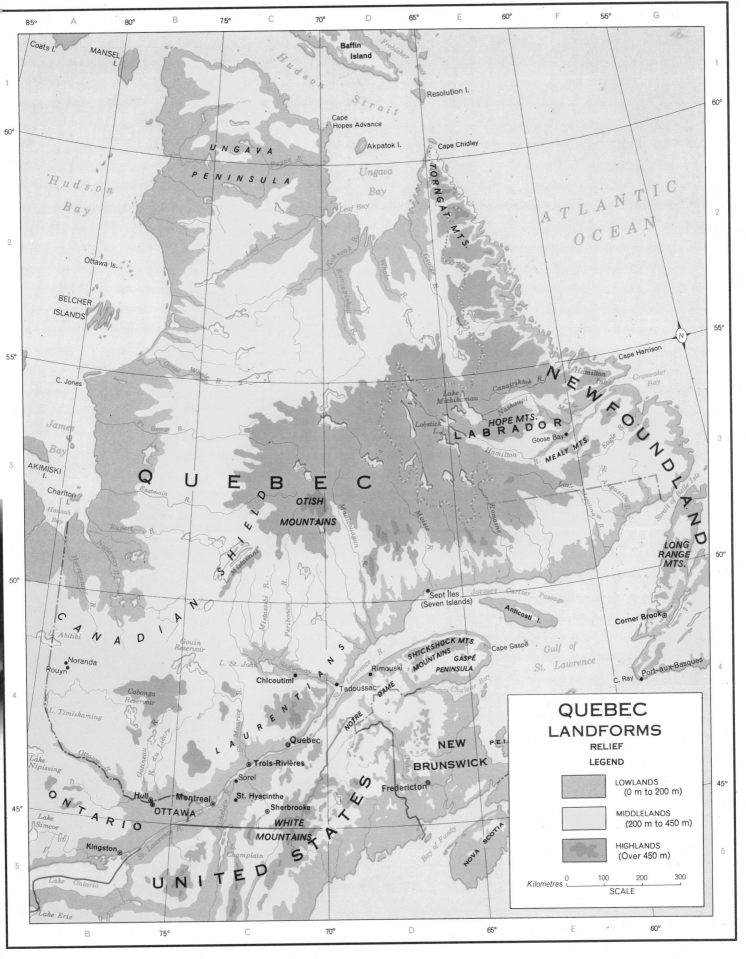

QUEBEC LANDFORMS

RELIEF

LEGEND

LOWLANDS
(0 m to 200 m)

MIDDLELANDS
(200 m to 450 m)

HIGHLANDS
(Over 450 m)

Kilometres   0   100   200   300

SCALE

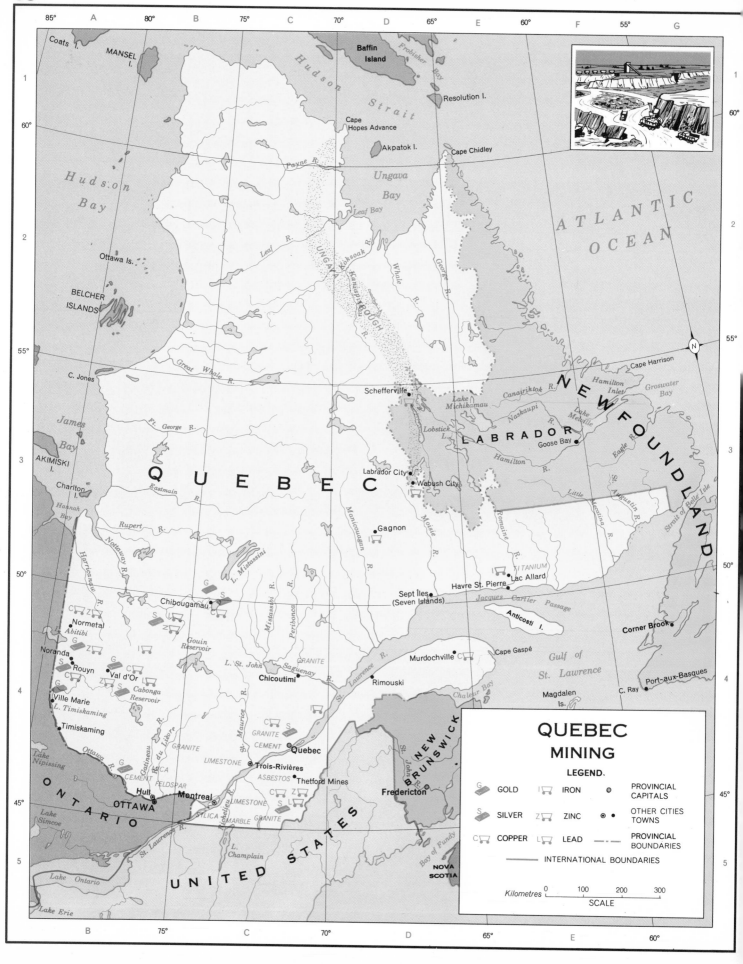

58

QUEBEC
MINING

LEGEND.

G	GOLD	I	IRON	●	PROVINCIAL CAPITALS
S	SILVER	Z	ZINC	⊙	OTHER CITIES TOWNS
C	COPPER	L	LEAD	— · —	PROVINCIAL BOUNDARIES
				—	INTERNATIONAL BOUNDARIES

Kilometres 0   100   200   300
SCALE

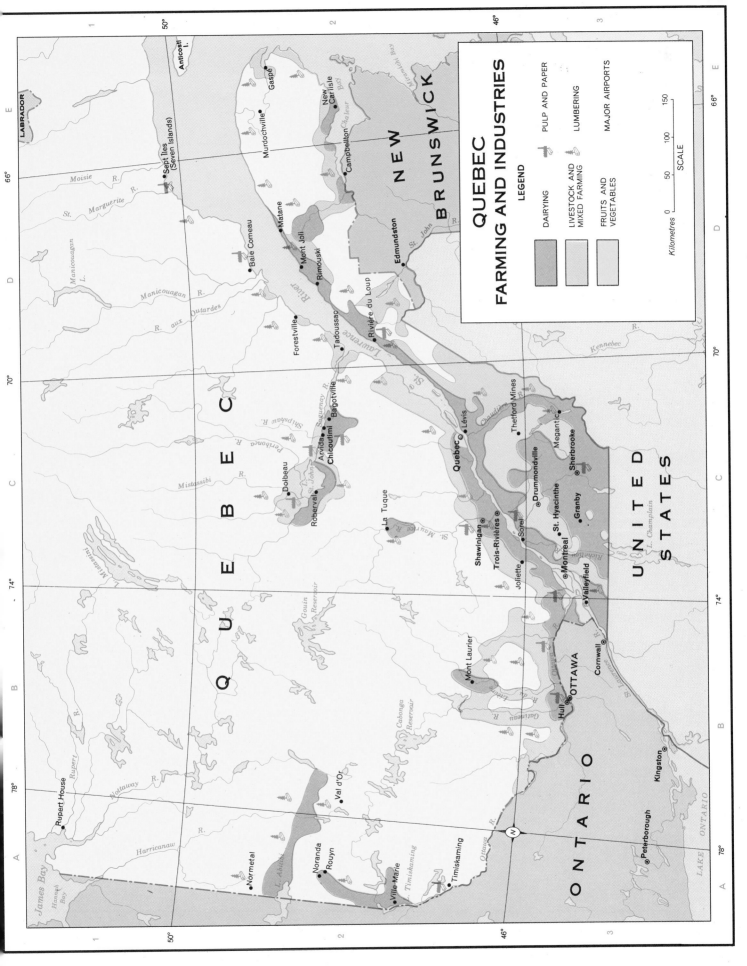

QUEBEC
FARMING AND INDUSTRIES

LEGEND

DAIRYING

LIVESTOCK AND
MIXED FARMING

FRUITS AND
VEGETABLES

PULP AND PAPER

LUMBERING

MAJOR AIRPORTS

Kilometres

0   50   100   150

SCALE

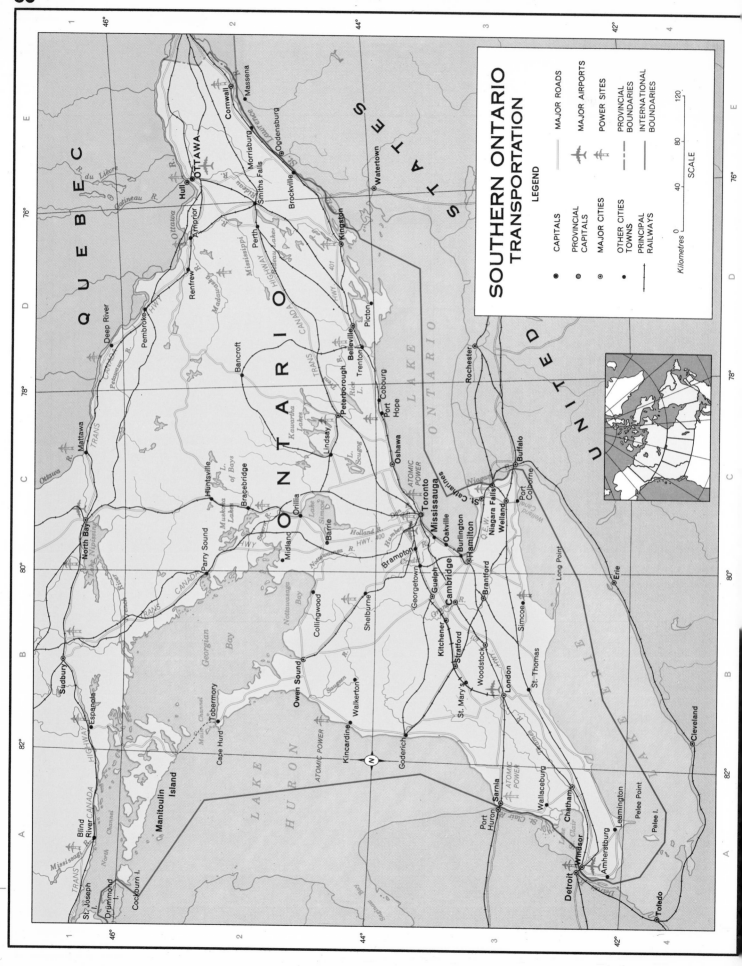

SOUTHERN ONTARIO TRANSPORTATION

LEGEND

CAPITALS ● CAPITALS

PROVINCIAL CAPITALS ◉ PROVINCIAL CAPITALS

MAJOR CITIES ◎ MAJOR CITIES

OTHER CITIES TOWNS • OTHER CITIES TOWNS

PRINCIPAL RAILWAYS ⊢⊣ PRINCIPAL RAILWAYS

—— MAJOR ROADS

✈ MAJOR AIRPORTS

◆ POWER SITES

—·—·— PROVINCIAL BOUNDARIES

—— INTERNATIONAL BOUNDARIES

SCALE

Kilometres

0   40   80   120

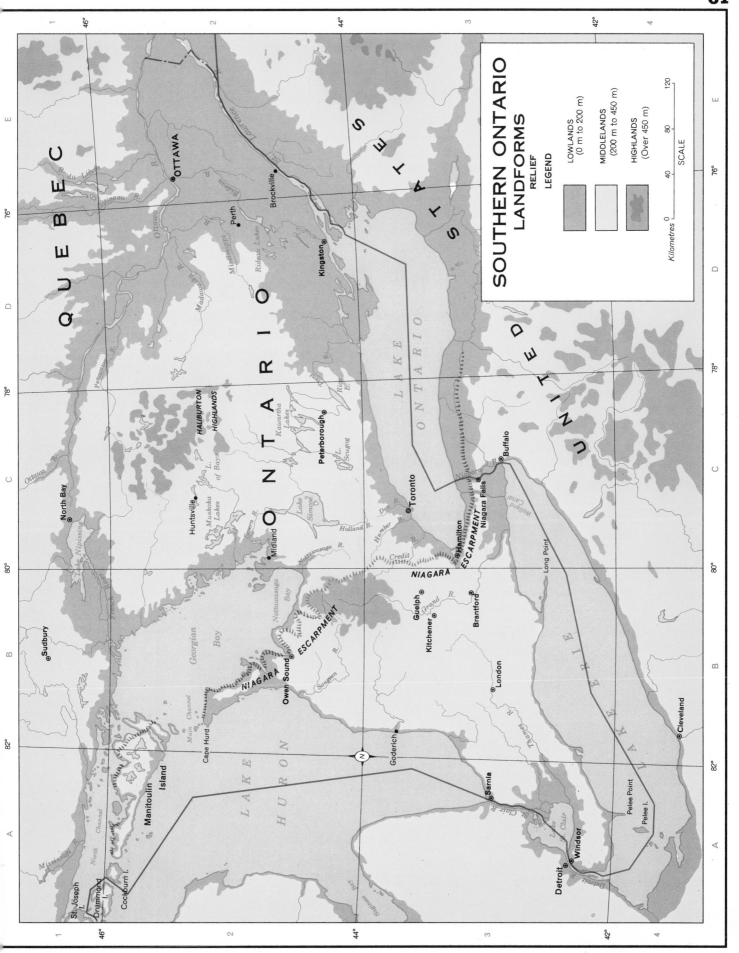

SOUTHERN ONTARIO LANDFORMS

RELIEF
LEGEND

LOWLANDS
(0 m to 200 m)

MIDDLELANDS
(200 m to 450 m)

HIGHLANDS
(Over 450 m)

SCALE

Kilometres 0   40   80   120

QUEBEC

ONTARIO

UNITED STATES

LAKE ONTARIO

LAKE ERIE

LAKE HURON

Georgian Bay

OTTAWA
Perth
Brockville
Kingston
Peterborough
North Bay
Huntsville
Midland
Toronto
Hamilton
Niagara Falls
Buffalo
Guelph
Kitchener
Brantford
London
Owen Sound
Goderich
Sarnia
Windsor
Detroit
Cleveland
Sudbury

HALIBURTON HIGHLANDS

NIAGARA ESCARPMENT
NIAGARA ESCARPMENT
NIAGARA ESCARPMENT

Manitoulin Island
St. Joseph I.
Drummond I.
Cockburn I.
Cape Hurd
Pelee Point
Pelee I.
Long Point

Ottawa R.
Gatineau R.
Rideau R.
Madawaska R.
Mississippi R.
Rideau Lakes
Kawartha Lakes
L. Scugog
Mushoka Lakes
Lake Simcoe
Holland R.
Humber R.
Don R.
Credit R.
Grand R.
Saugeen R.
Thames R.
Nottawasaga R.
Nottawasaga Bay
Lake Nipissing
L. of Bays
St. Clair R.
Lake St. Clair
Detroit R.
Welland Canal
Niagara R.
North Channel
Main Channel
Petawawa R.

N

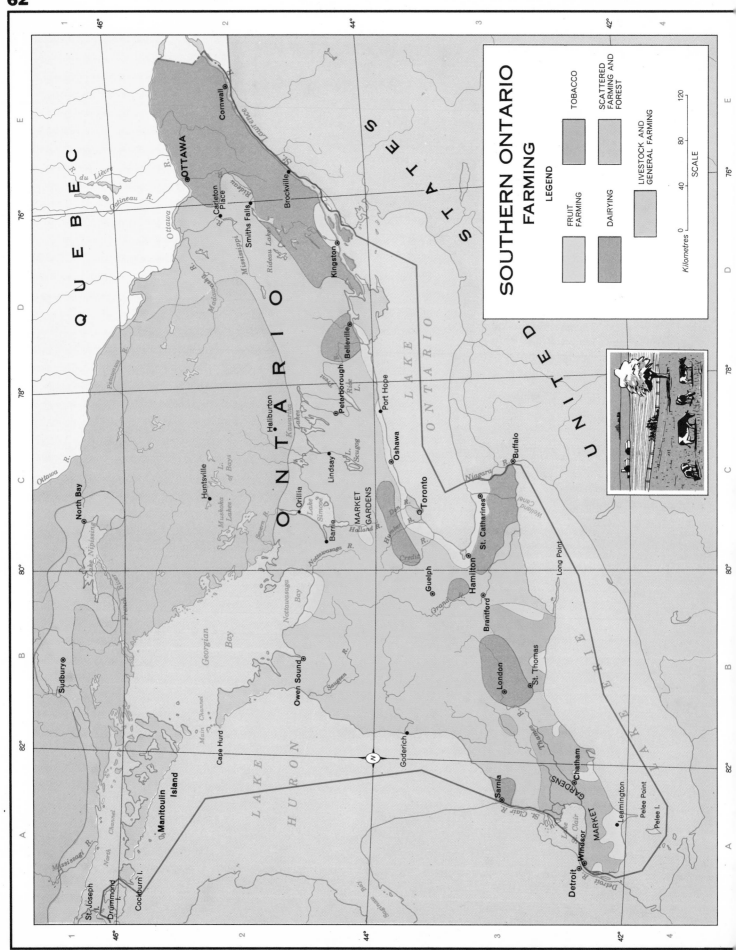

SOUTHERN ONTARIO
FARMING

LEGEND

FRUIT FARMING

TOBACCO

DAIRYING

SCATTERED FARMING AND FOREST

LIVESTOCK AND GENERAL FARMING

SCALE

Kilometres 0   40   80   120

QUEBEC

O N T A R I O

U N I T E D   S T A T E S

LAKE ONTARIO

LAKE ERIE

LAKE HURON

Georgian Bay

Nottawasaga Bay

Lake Nipissing

du Lièvre
Gatineau R.
Ottawa R.
Mississippi R.
Madawaska R.
Petawawa R.
Rideau Lake
Rideau R.
Trent R.
Kawartha Lakes
L. Scugog
Severn R.
Holland R.
Nottawasaga R.
Saugeen R.
Maitland R.
Grand R.
Thames R.
St. Clair R.
Detroit R.
Niagara R.
Welland Canal
Credit R.
Humber R.
Don R.
L. Simcoe
L. of Bays
Muskoka Lakes
French R.
North Channel
Main Channel
Mississagi R.
Sydenham R.
Long Point
Lake St. Clair

St. Lawrence R.
Cataraqui R.

Cornwall
OTTAWA
Carleton Place
Smiths Falls
Brockville
Kingston
Belleville
Peterborough
Port Hope
Haliburton
Halibut
Oshawa
Lindsay
Orillia
Barrie
Toronto
St. Catharines
Buffalo
Guelph
Hamilton
Brantford
London
St. Thomas
Owen Sound
Huntsville
North Bay
Sudbury
Cape Hurd
Goderich
Sarnia
Chatham
Leamington
Pelee Point
Pelee I.
Windsor
Detroit
Manitoulin Island
St. Joseph I.
Drummond I.
Cockburn I.

MARKET GARDENS
MARKET GARDENS

63

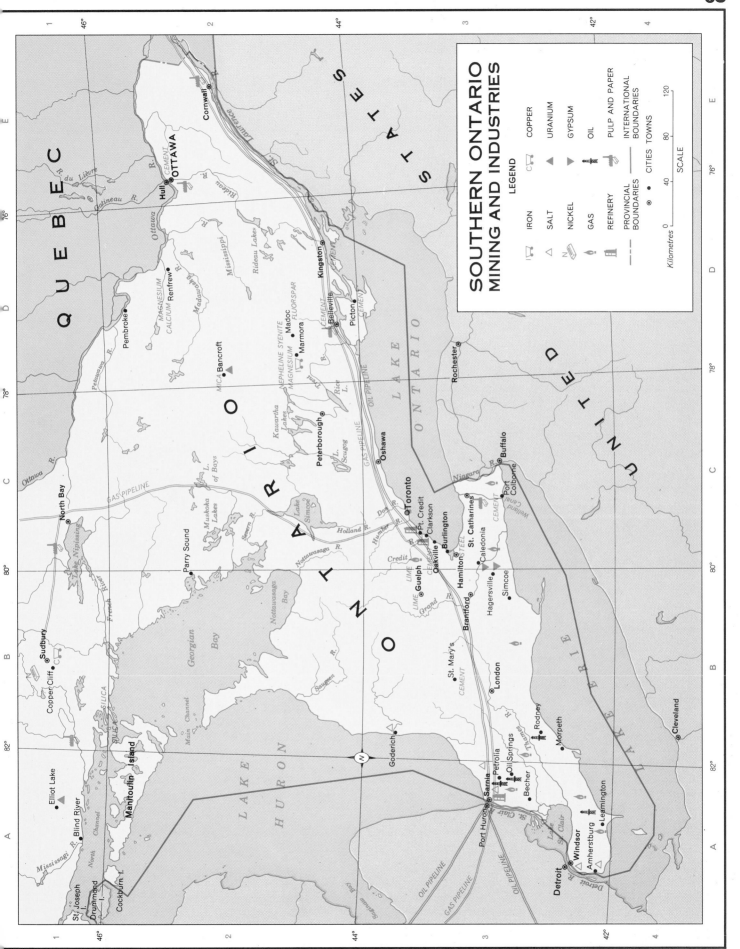

SOUTHERN ONTARIO MINING AND INDUSTRIES

LEGEND

IRON · COPPER
SALT · URANIUM
NICKEL · GYPSUM
GAS · OIL
REFINERY · PULP AND PAPER
PROVINCIAL BOUNDARIES · INTERNATIONAL BOUNDARIES
CITIES · TOWNS

SCALE
Kilometres 0 40 80 120

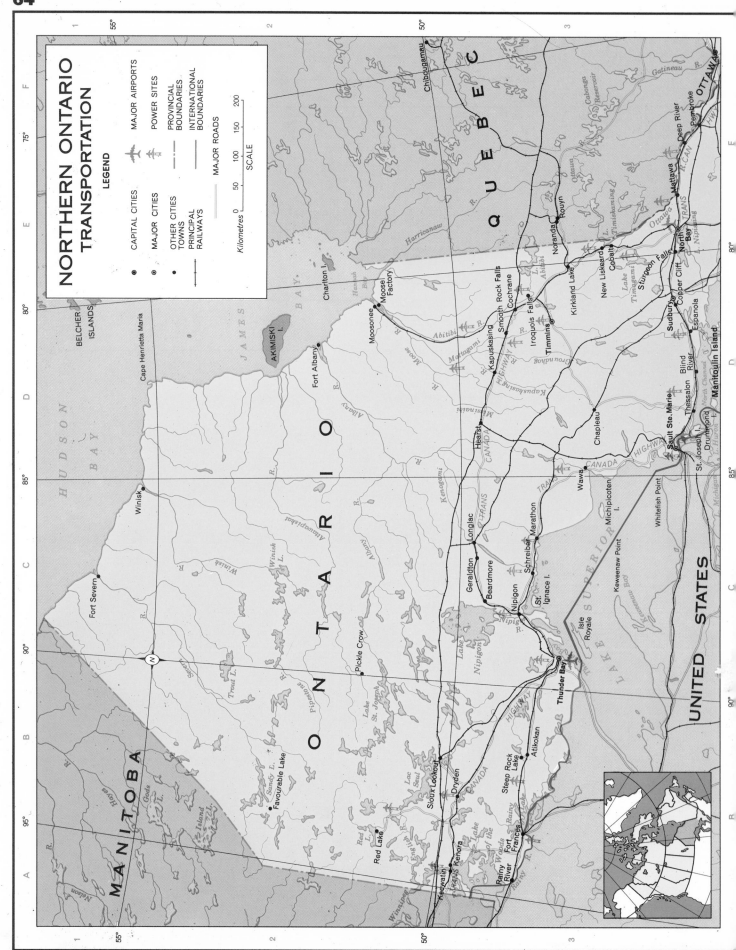

NORTHERN ONTARIO TRANSPORTATION

LEGEND

●	CAPITAL CITIES	✈ MAJOR AIRPORTS
◉	MAJOR CITIES	✈ POWER SITES
•	OTHER CITIES TOWNS	—·—·— PROVINCIAL BOUNDARIES
	PRINCIPAL RAILWAYS	— — — INTERNATIONAL BOUNDARIES
		—— MAJOR ROADS

SCALE

Kilometres 0 50 100 150 200

QUEBEC

ONTARIO

MANITOBA

UNITED STATES

HUDSON BAY

JAMES BAY

LAKE SUPERIOR

BELCHER ISLANDS

AKIMISKI I.

Charlton I.

Cape Henrietta Maria

Winisk

Fort Severn

Fort Albany

Moosonee

Moose Factory

Chibougamau

Red Lake

Favourable Lake

Pickle Crow

Sioux Lookout

Dryden

Kenora

Keewatin

Fort Frances

Rainy River

Atikokan

Steep Rock Lake

Thunder Bay

Nipigon

St. Ignace I.

Schreiber

Beardmore

Geraldton

Longlac

Marathon

Wawa

Michipicoten I.

Whitefish Point

Keweenaw Point

Isle Royale

Hearst

Chapleau

Kapuskasing

Smooth Rock Falls

Cochrane

Iroquois Falls

Timmins

Kirkland Lake

New Liskeard

Cobalt

Noranda

Rouyn

Sudbury

Copper Cliff

Espanola

Blind River

Thessalon

Sault Ste. Marie

St. Joseph I.

Drummond I.

Manitoulin Island

Sturgeon Falls

North Bay

Mattawa

Deep River

Pembroke

OTTAWA

TRANS CANADA HIGHWAY

HUDSON BAY

Gods L.

Island L.

Sandy L.

Trout L.

Lake St. Joseph

Lac Seul

Red L.

Lake of the Woods

Rainy Lake

Winisk L.

Attawapiskat R.

Albany R.

Kenogami R.

Lake Nipigon

Nipigon R.

Abitibi L.

Timiskaming L.

Lake Timagami

Lake Nipissing

Gatineau R.

Ottawa R.

Cabonga Reservoir

Harricanaw R.

Moose R.

Abitibi R.

Mattagami R.

Missinaibi R.

Groundhog R.

Kapuskasing R.

Nelson R.

Hayes R.

Winnipeg R.

English R.

Rainy R.

Winisk R.

Severn R.

Hope R.

Pipestone R.

Albany R.

Winnipeg L.

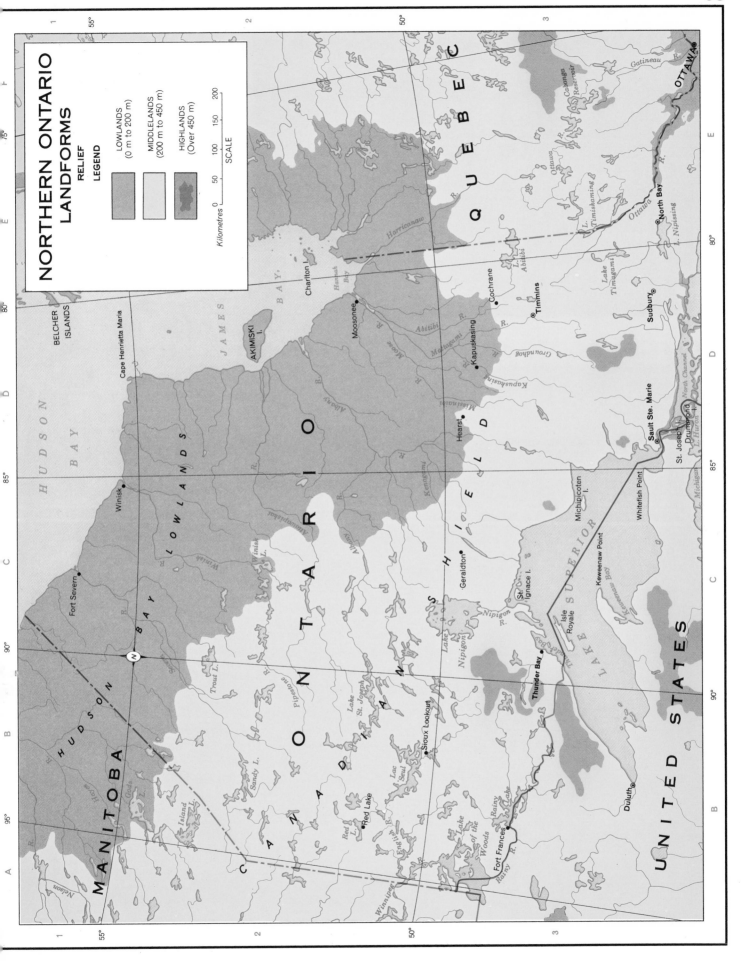

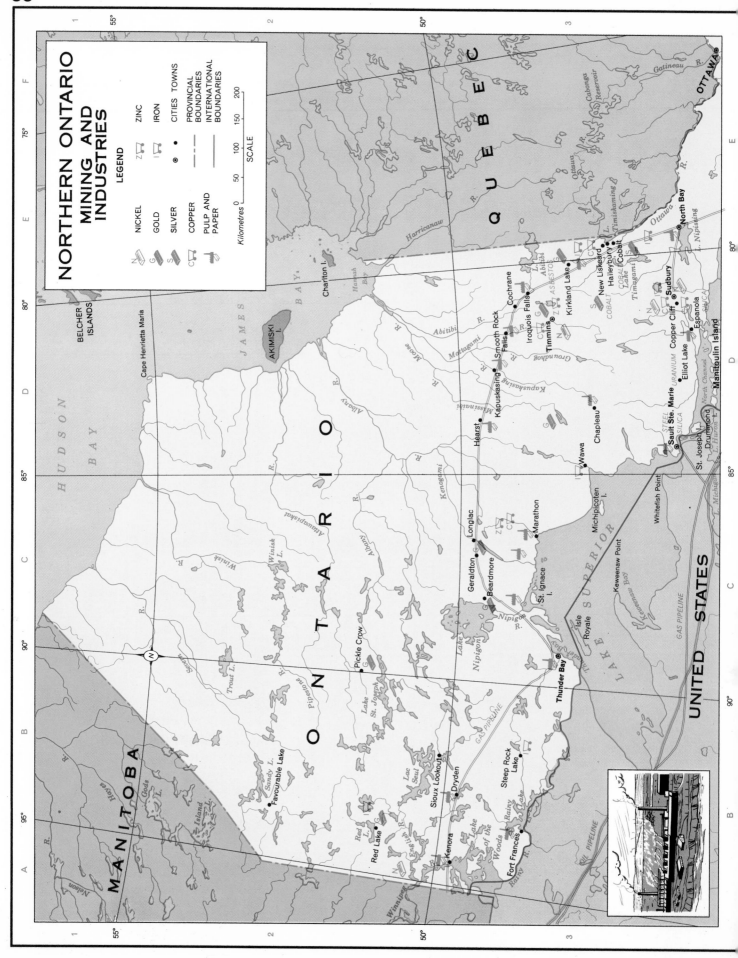

66

NORTHERN ONTARIO
MINING AND INDUSTRIES

LEGEND

NICKEL N

GOLD G

SILVER S

COPPER C

PULP AND PAPER

ZINC Z

IRON I

● CITIES TOWNS

⊙ CITIES TOWNS

PROVINCIAL BOUNDARIES

INTERNATIONAL BOUNDARIES

Kilometres

0   50   100   150   200

SCALE

HUDSON   BAY

BELCHER ISLANDS

Cape Henrietta Maria

JAMES   BAY

Charlton I.

Hannah Bay

AKIMISKI I.

MANITOBA

Nelson R.

Hayes R.

Gods L.

Island L.

Severn R.

Sandy L.

Favourable Lake

Winisk L.

Winisk R.

Attawapiskat R.

Pipestone R.

Trout L.

Red L.

Red Lake

English R.

Lac Seul

Lake of the Woods

Kenora

Sioux Lookout

Dryden

Fort Frances

Rainy L.

Rainy R.

ONTARIO

Pickle Crow G

Lake St. Joseph

Albany R.

Albany R.

Winisk R.

Kenogami R.

Ogoki R.

Lake Nipigon

Nipigon R.

Nipigon

Geraldton G

Beardmore G

Longlac

Steep Rock Lake I

Thunder Bay

GAS PIPELINE

OIL PIPELINE

Moose R.

Abitibi R.

Mattagami R.

Missinaibi R.

Groundhog R.

Kapuskasing R.

Hearst

Kapuskasing

Smooth Rock Falls

Cochrane

Iroquois Falls

Timmins ⊙

Kirkland Lake G

ASBESTOS

L. Abitibi

Chapleau G

Wawa I

Marathon Z C

St. Ignace I.

Michipicoten I.

LAKE   SUPERIOR

Isle Royale

Keweenaw Point

Keweenaw Bay

Whitefish Point

GAS PIPELINE

UNITED STATES

Sault Ste. Marie

STEEL

SILICA

URANIUM

Elliot Lake

St. Joseph I.

Drummond I.

North Channel

Manitoulin Island

Lake Huron

Espanola

Copper Cliff

Sudbury ●

N

New Liskeard

Haileybury

COBALT

Cobalt

Timagami

L. Timiskaming

North Bay ●

L. Nipissing

Ottawa R.

OTTAWA

Gatineau R.

Cabonga Reservoir

QUEBEC

Harricanaw R.

Ottawa R.

Mattawa R.

R.

R.

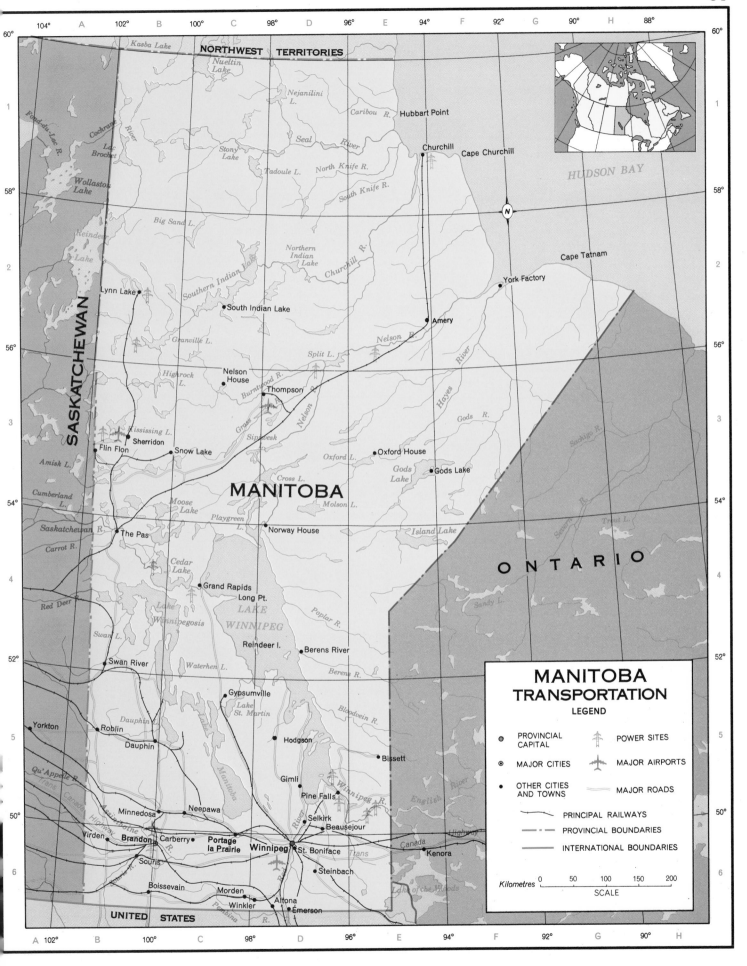

NORTHWEST TERRITORIES

Kasba Lake

Nueltin Lake

Nejanilini L.

Caribou R. Hubbart Point

Fond-du-Lac R.

Cochrane River

Lac Brochet

Wollaston Lake

Stony Lake

Seal *River*

Churchill Cape Churchill

Tadoule L. *North Knife R.*

South Knife R.

HUDSON BAY

N

Reindeer Lake

Big Sand L.

Northern Indian Lake

Churchill R.

Cape Tatnam

Lynn Lake

Southern Indian Lake

York Factory

Granville L.

Amery

Nelson R.

South Indian Lake

Highrock L.

Nelson House

Split L.

Hayes River

Gods R.

Sachigo R.

Kississing L. Thompson

Burntwood R.

Sherridon

Groos *Nelson*

Sipiwesk L.

Flin Flon Snow Lake

MANITOBA

Oxford L. Oxford House

Gods Lake Gods Lake

Amisk L.

Cross L.

Molson L.

Cumberland L.

Moose Lake

ONTARIO

Saskatchewan R. The Pas

Playgreen L. Norway House

Island Lake

Sawn R.

Trout L.

Carrot R.

Cedar Lake

Red Deer

Grand Rapids

Long Pt.

Lake Winnipegosis

LAKE WINNIPEG

Poplar R.

Sandy L.

Swan L.

Reindeer I.

Berens River

Swan River

Waterhen L.

Berens R.

Bloodvein R.

Gypsumville

Lake St. Martin

English River

Yorkton

Roblin

Hodgson

Dauphin *L.*

Bissett

Dauphin L.

Dauphin

Gimli

Pine Falls

Winnipeg R.

Minnedosa

Neepawa

Selkirk

Qu'Appelle R.

Trans Canada Highway

Assiniboine

Beausejour

Virden Brandon Carberry

Portage la Prairie

Winnipeg St. Boniface

River

Kenora

Souris

Trans Canada Highway

Boissevain

Steinbach

Lake of the Woods

Morden

Souris R.

Winkler Altona

UNITED STATES *Pembina R.* Emerson

MANITOBA TRANSPORTATION

LEGEND

⊚ PROVINCIAL CAPITAL	⚡ POWER SITES
⊙ MAJOR CITIES	✈ MAJOR AIRPORTS
• OTHER CITIES AND TOWNS	≈ MAJOR ROADS

PRINCIPAL RAILWAYS

PROVINCIAL BOUNDARIES

INTERNATIONAL BOUNDARIES

Kilometres 0 50 100 150 200

SCALE

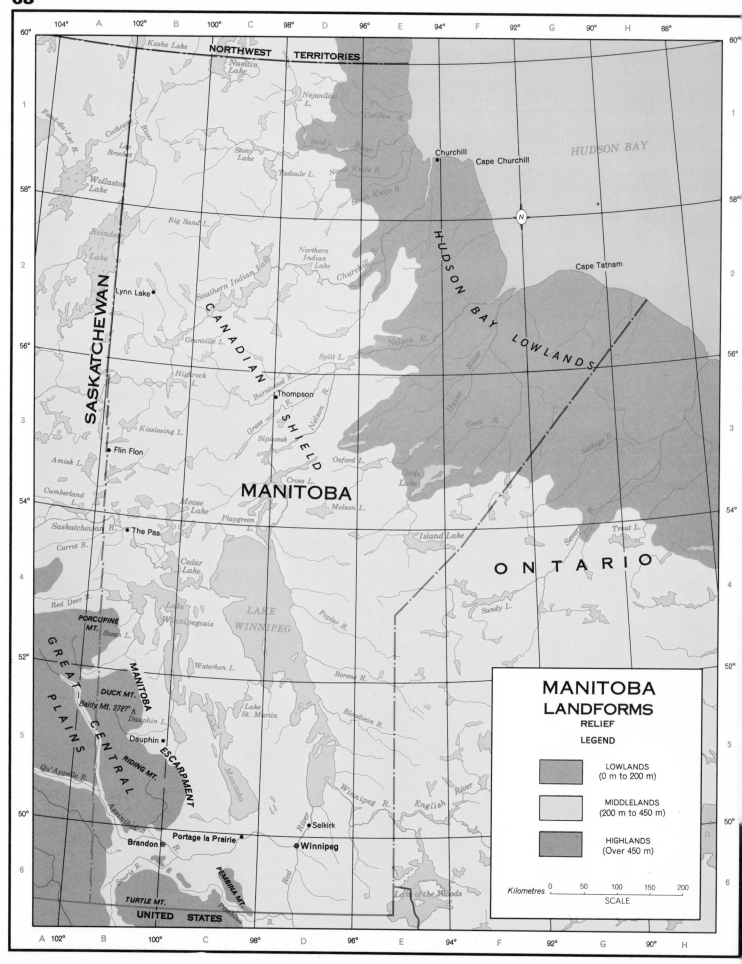

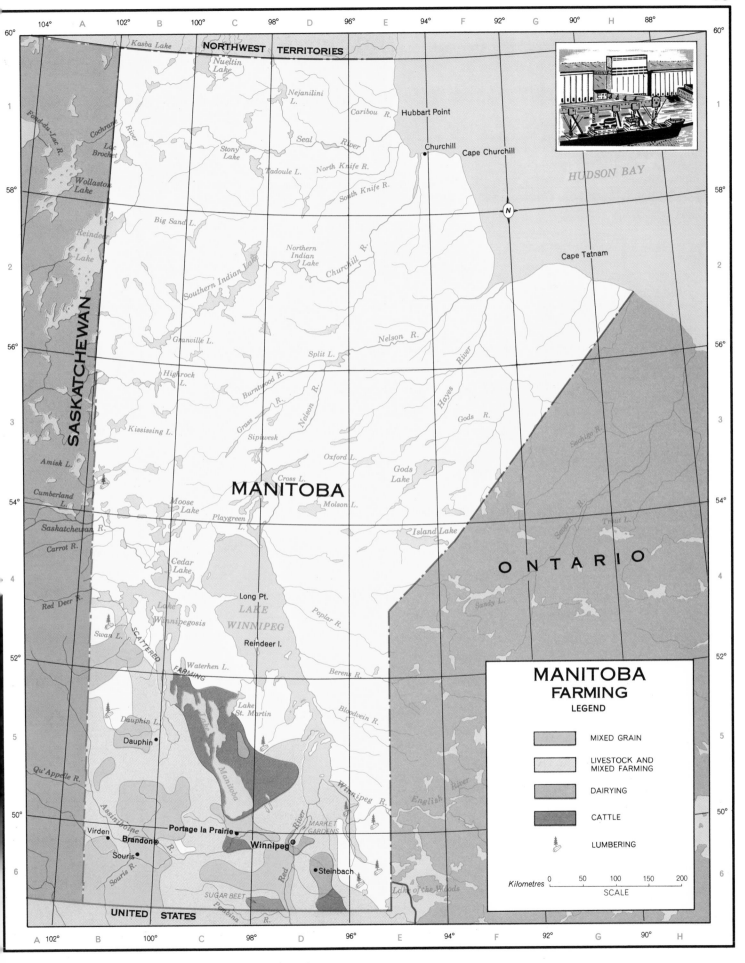

60°

104° | A | 102° | B | 100° | C | 98° | D | 96° | E | 94° | F | 92° | G | 90° | H | 88°

Kasba Lake

NORTHWEST TERRITORIES

Nueltin Lake

Nejanilini L.

Caribou R.

Hubbart Point

Seal

Stony Lake

River

Churchill

Cape Churchill

Tadoule L.

North Knife R.

HUDSON BAY

South Knife R.

Big Sand L.

Reindeer Lake

Northern Indian Lake

Cape Tatnam

Southern Indian Lake

Churchill R.

N

Granville L.

Nelson R.

Split L.

River

Highrock L.

Burntwood R.

Hayes

Nelson R.

Gods R.

Kississing L.

Grass

Sipiwesk

R.

Sachigo R.

Amisk L.

Oxford L.

Gods Lake

Cumberland L.

Cross L.

MANITOBA

Molson L.

Saskatchewan R.

Moose Lake

Playgreen L.

Island Lake

Segura R.

Trout L.

Carrot R.

Cedar Lake

ONTARIO

Red Deer R.

Lake Winnipegosis

Long Pt.

LAKE WINNIPEG

Poplar R.

Sandy L.

Swan L.

SCATTERED

Dauphin L.

Reindeer I.

FARMING

Waterhen L.

Berens R.

Dauphin

Lake St. Martin

Lake Manitoba

Bloodvein R.

Qu'Appelle R.

Winnipeg R.

English

River

Assiniboine

Virden

Portage la Prairie

MARKET GARDENS

Brandon

River

Red

Souris

Winnipeg

River

Steinbach

Souris R.

SUGAR BEET

Pembina R.

Lake of the Woods

UNITED STATES

102° | B | 100° | C | 98° | D | 96° | E | 94° | F | 92° | G | 90° | H

MANITOBA
FARMING
LEGEND

- MIXED GRAIN
- LIVESTOCK AND MIXED FARMING
- DAIRYING
- CATTLE
- LUMBERING

Kilometres 0 50 100 150 200

SCALE

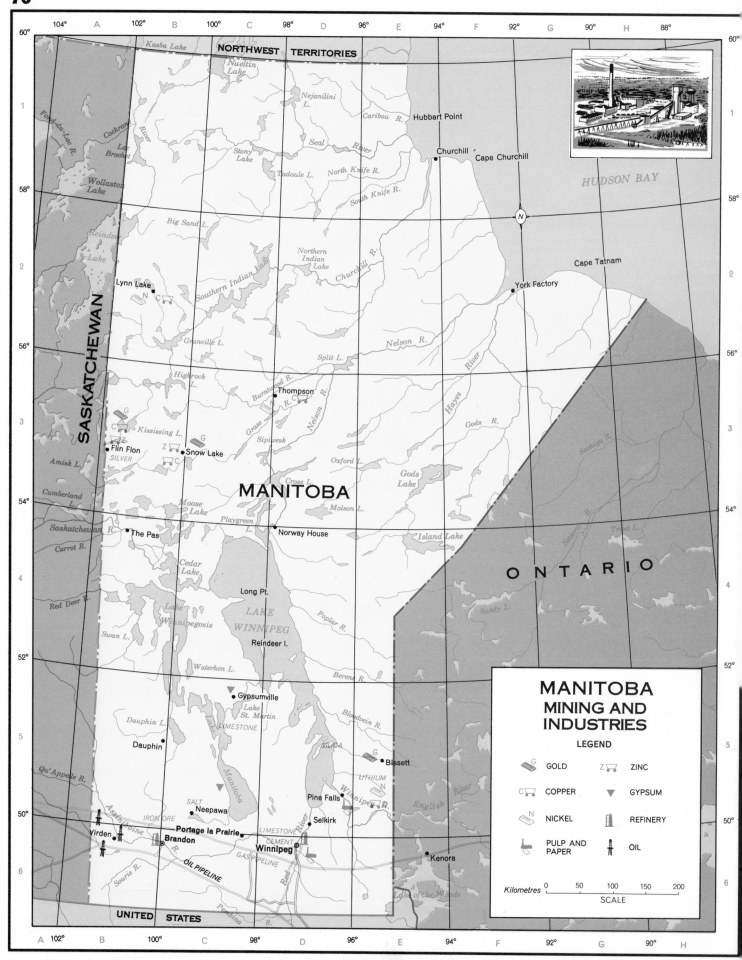

104° A 102° B 100° C 98° D 96° E 94° F 92° G 90° H 88°

60°

NORTHWEST   TERRITORIES

Kasba Lake

Nueltin Lake

Fond-du-Lac R.

Cochrane River

Lac Brochet

1

Nejanilini L.

Caribou R.

Hubbart Point

Wollaston Lake

Stony Lake

Tadoule L.

North Knife R.

Churchill

Cape Churchill

58°

Reindeer Lake

Big Sand L.

Seal   *River*

South Knife R.

HUDSON BAY

N

2

Lynn Lake 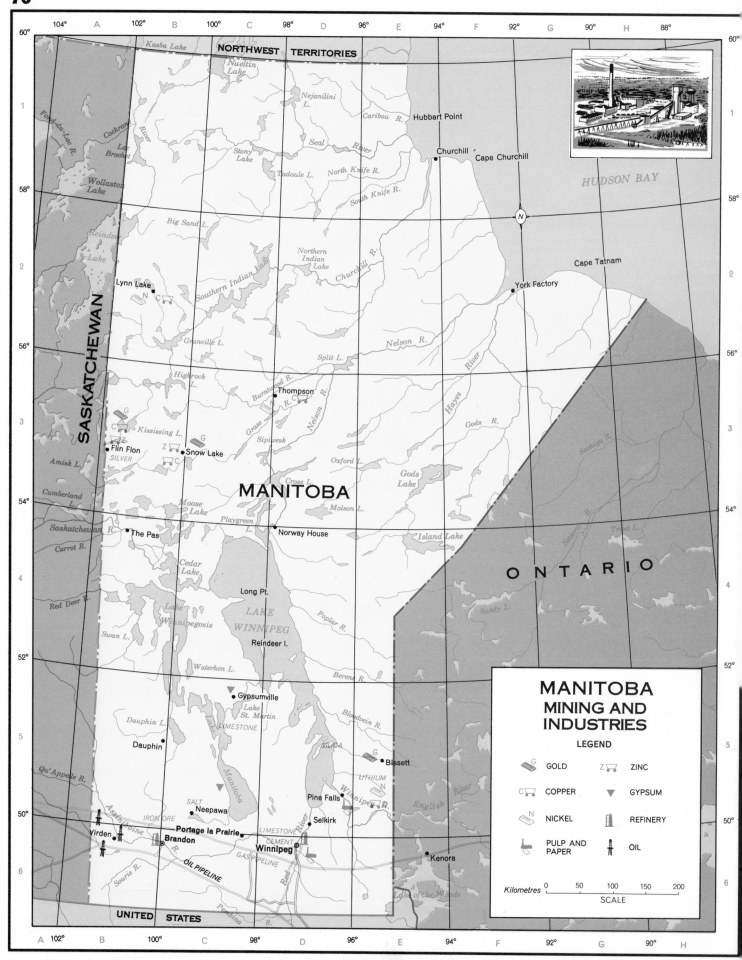 N C

Southern Indian Lake

Northern Indian Lake

Cape Tatnam

York Factory

Granville L.

Churchill R.

56°

Highrock L.

Burntwood R.

Thompson C

Split L.

Nelson R.

Hayes River

SASKATCHEWAN

G

3

C

Z

SILVER

Kississing L.

Z

Flin Flon

G

C

Snow Lake

Grass R.

Sipiwesk

Nelson R.

Gods R.

Oxford L.

Gods Lake

Amisk L.

Cumberland L.

MANITOBA

Cross L.

54°

Saskatchewan R.

Carrot R.

Moose Lake

The Pas

Playgreen L.

Norway House

Molson L.

Island Lake

Sachigo R.

ONTARIO

Severn River

Trout L.

4

Red Deer R.

Cedar Lake

Long Pt.

Lake Winnipegosis

LAKE WINNIPEG

Poplar R.

Sandy L.

Swan L.

52°

Reindeer I.

Waterhen L.

Berens R.

Bloodvein R.

Gypsumville

Lake St. Martin

LIMESTONE

Dauphin L.

SILICA

5

Dauphin

G

Bissett

LITHIUM

N

Winnipeg R.

50°

SALT

Neepawa

Pine Falls

IRON ORE

Virden

Portage la Prairie

Brandon

Selkirk

LIMESTONE

CEMENT

Winnipeg

Assiniboine R.

Qu'Appelle R.

Souris R.

OIL PIPELINE

GAS PIPELINE

Red River

Lake of the Woods

Kenora

6

UNITED   STATES

Pembina R.

A 102° B 100° C 98° D 96° E 94° F 92° G 90° H

MANITOBA
MINING AND
INDUSTRIES

LEGEND

G GOLD   Z ZINC

C COPPER   GYPSUM

N NICKEL   REFINERY

PULP AND   OIL
PAPER

Kilometres 0   50   100   150   200

SCALE

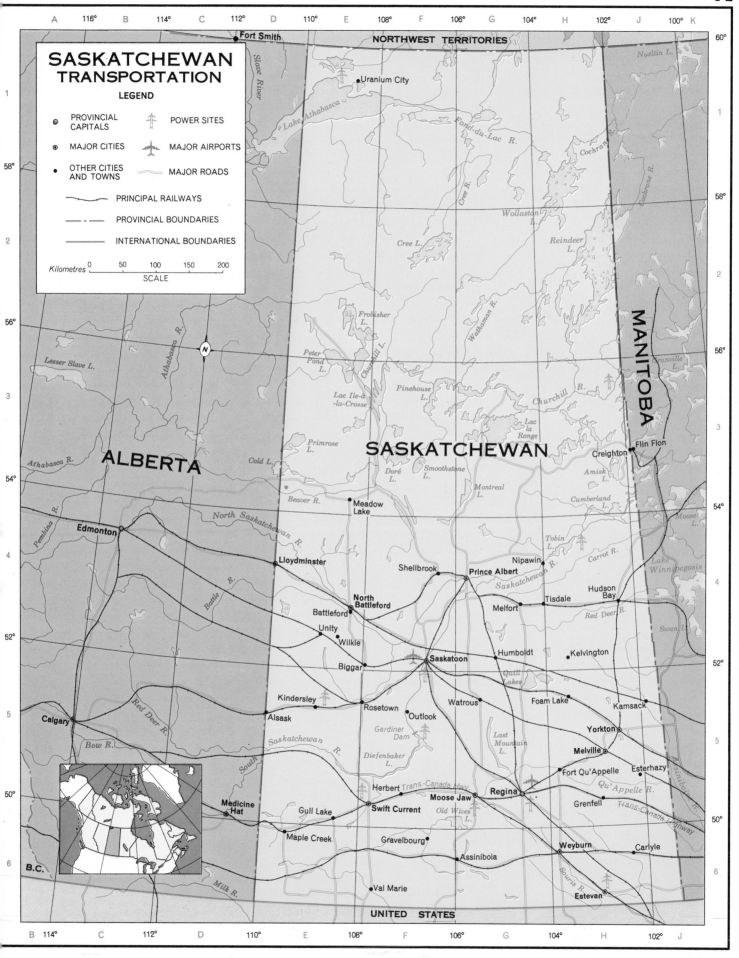

SASKATCHEWAN
TRANSPORTATION
LEGEND

- ◉ PROVINCIAL CAPITALS
- ◎ MAJOR CITIES
- ● OTHER CITIES AND TOWNS
- ⚡ POWER SITES
- ✈ MAJOR AIRPORTS
- 〰 MAJOR ROADS
- 〜 PRINCIPAL RAILWAYS
- — · — PROVINCIAL BOUNDARIES
- ——— INTERNATIONAL BOUNDARIES

Kilometres 0 50 100 150 200
SCALE

NORTHWEST TERRITORIES

Fort Smith

Uranium City

Nueltin L.

Slave River

Lake Athabasca

Fond-du-Lac R.

Cochrane R.

Cree R.

Wollaston L.

Cree L.

Reindeer L.

Wahaman R.

MANITOBA

Frobisher L.

Peter Pond L.

Lac Ile-à-la-Crosse

Churchill L.

Pinehouse L.

Churchill R.

Lesser Slave L.

Athabaska R.

N

Primrose L.

Doré L.

Smoothstone L.

Lac la Ronge

Granville L.

SASKATCHEWAN

Creighton

Flin Flon

Amisk L.

Athabasca R.

Cold L.

Montreal L.

Cumberland L.

Moose L.

ALBERTA

Beaver R.

Meadow Lake

North Saskatchewan R.

Tobin L.

Lake Winnipegosis

Edmonton

Pembina R.

Lloydminster

Shellbrook

Prince Albert

Nipawin

Carrot R.

Hudson Bay

Swan L.

Battle R.

North Battleford

Melfort

Tisdale

Red Deer R.

Battleford

Saskatchewan R.

Unity

Wilkie

Humboldt

Kelvington

Saskatoon

Biggar

Quill Lakes

Calgary

Kindersley

Rosetown

Watrous

Foam Lake

Kamsack

Red Deer R.

Alsask

Outlook

Yorkton

Bow R.

Saskatchewan R.

Gardiner Dam

Last Mountain L.

Melville

Esterhazy

Diefenbaker L.

Fort Qu'Appelle

Qu'Appelle R.

Trans-Canada Hwy.

Herbert

Regina

Grenfell

Trans-Canada Highway

Medicine Hat

Gull Lake

Swift Current

Moose Jaw

Old Wives L.

Maple Creek

Gravelbourg

Weyburn

Carlyle

Souris R.

B.C.

Milk R.

Val Marie

Assiniboia

Estevan

UNITED STATES

116° 114° 112° 110° 108° 106° 104° 102° 100°

114° 112° 110° 108° 106° 104° 102°

60° 58° 56° 54° 52° 50°

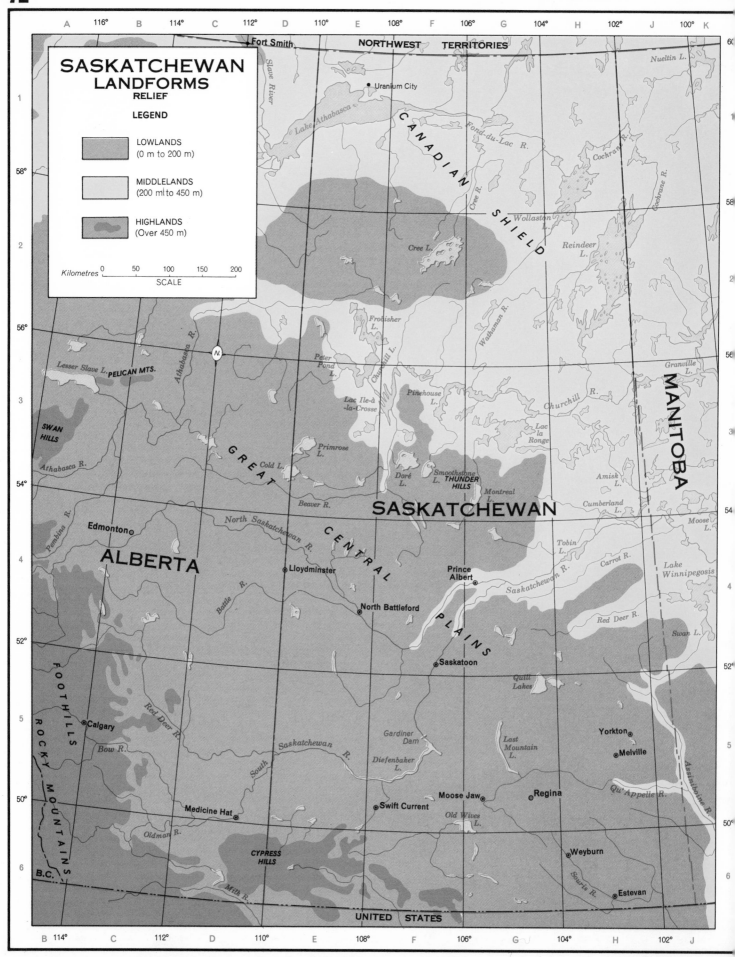

SASKATCHEWAN LANDFORMS
RELIEF

LEGEND

LOWLANDS
(0 m to 200 m)

MIDDLELANDS
(200 ml to 450 m)

HIGHLANDS
(Over 450 m)

Kilometres 0   50   100   150   200
SCALE

Fort Smith

NORTHWEST   TERRITORIES

Nueltin L.

Uranium City

Lake Athabasca

Slave River

CANADIAN   SHIELD

Fond-du-Lac R.

Cochran R.

Cree R.

Wollaston L.

Cochrane R.

Cree L.

Reindeer L.

Frobisher L.

Washaman R.

Peter Pond L.

Churchill R.

Granville L.

MANITOBA

Lesser Slave L.   PELICAN MTS.

Lac Ile-à -la-Crosse

Pinehouse L.

Churchill R.

Athabasca R.

N.

SWAN HILLS

Primrose L.

Lac la Ronge

Amisk L.

Athabasca R.

GREAT

Cold L.

Doré L.

Smoothstone L.   THUNDER HILLS

Montreal L.

Cumberland L.

Moose L.

Beaver R.

SASKATCHEWAN

Pembina R.

Edmonton

North Saskatchewan R.

CENTRAL

Tobin L.

Carrot R.

Lake Winnipegosis

ALBERTA

Lloydminster

Prince Albert

Saskatchewan R.

Battle R.

North Battleford

PLAINS

Red Deer R.

Swan L.

FOOTHILLS

Saskatoon

Quill Lakes

ROCKY

Calgary

Red Deer R.

Gardiner Dam

Last Mountain L.

Yorkton

Bow R.

Diefenbaker L.

Melville

MOUNTAINS

South   Saskatchewan   R.

Moose Jaw

Regina

Qu'Appelle R.

Assiniboine R.

B.C.

Medicine Hat

Swift Current

Old Wives L.

50°

Oldman R.

Weyburn

CYPRESS HILLS

Souris R.

Estevan

Milk R.

UNITED   STATES

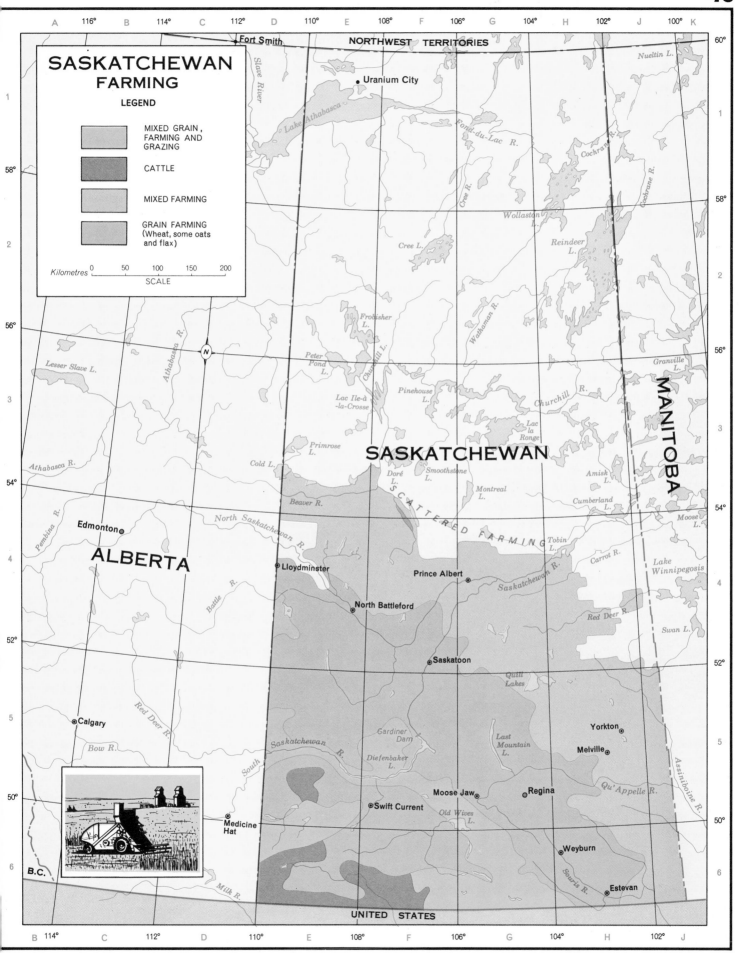

SASKATCHEWAN
FARMING

LEGEND

MIXED GRAIN,
FARMING AND
GRAZING

CATTLE

MIXED FARMING

GRAIN FARMING
(Wheat, some oats
and flax)

Kilometres 0   50   100   150   200

SCALE

NORTHWEST TERRITORIES

Fort Smith

• Uranium City

Slave River

Lake Athabasca

Nueltin L.

Fond-du-Lac R.

Cochrane R.

Cree R.

Wollaston L.

Cree L.

Reindeer L.

Cochrane R.

MANITOBA

Frobisher L.

Wathaman R.

Peter Pond L.

Churchill L.

Pinehouse L.

Churchill R.

Granville L.

Lac Ile-à-la-Crosse

Lac la Ronge

Amisk L.

Athabasca R.

N

SASKATCHEWAN

Doré L.

Smoothstone

Cumberland L.

Moose L.

Lesser Slave L.

Beaver R.

Montreal L.

SCATTERED FARMING

Tobin L.

Athabasca R.

North Saskatchewan R.

Carrot R.

Lake Winnipegosis

Edmonton ⊙

ALBERTA

Lloydminster ⊙

Prince Albert ⊙

Saskatchewan R.

Red Deer R.

Battle R.

North Battleford ⊙

Swan L.

Pembina R.

Saskatoon ⊙

Quill Lakes

Red Deer R.

Gardiner Dam

Last Mountain L.

Yorkton ⊙

Calgary ⊙

Saskatchewan R.

Diefenbaker L.

Melville ⊙

Bow R.

South Saskatchewan R.

Moose Jaw ⊙

Regina ⊙

Qu'Appelle R.

Assiniboine R.

Medicine Hat ⊙

Swift Current ⊙

Old Wives L.

Weyburn ⊙

B.C.

Milk R.

Souris R.

Estevan ⊙

UNITED STATES

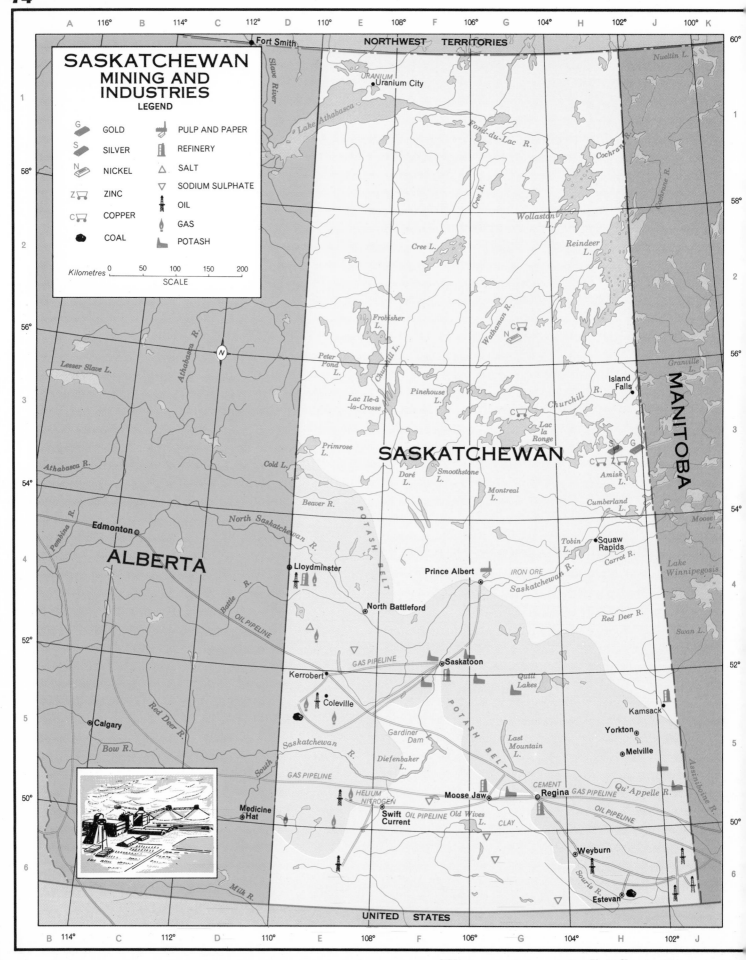

SASKATCHEWAN
MINING AND INDUSTRIES
LEGEND

G GOLD
S SILVER
N NICKEL
Z ZINC
C COPPER
COAL

PULP AND PAPER
REFINERY
SALT
SODIUM SULPHATE
OIL
GAS
POTASH

Kilometres 0 50 100 150 200
SCALE

NORTHWEST TERRITORIES

Fort Smith

Slave River

Lake Athabasca

URANIUM
Uranium City

Fond-du-Lac R.

Nueltin L.

Cochrane R.

Cree R.

Wollaston L.

Cree L.

Reindeer L.

Wathaman R.
N C

Frobisher L.

Peter Pond L.

Pinehouse L.

Churchill R.

Island Falls

Granville L.

SASKATCHEWAN

Lac Ile-à -la-Crosse

Lac la Ronge

C

Amisk L.

S G
C Z

Cumberland L.

Moose L.

Primrose L.

Cold L.

Doré L.

Smoothstone L.

Montreal L.

MANITOBA

Athabasca R.

Lesser Slave L.

Beaver R.

North Saskatchewan R.

Edmonton

Tobin L.

Squaw Rapids

Lake Winnipegosis

ALBERTA

Lloydminster

Prince Albert

IRON ORE

Saskatchewan R.

Carrot R.

Red Deer R.

Swan L.

North Battleford

POTASH BELT

Battle R.

OIL PIPELINE

Saskatoon

Qutti Lakes

Kamsack

Pembina R.

Red Deer R.

GAS PIPELINE

Kerrobert

Coleville

Yorkton

Calgary

Gardiner Dam

Last Mountain L.

Melville

Bow R.

Saskatchewan R.

Diefenbaker L.

POTASH BELT

Qu'Appelle R.

Assiniboine R.

GAS PIPELINE

South Saskatchewan R.

CEMENT

Moose Jaw

Regina
GAS PIPELINE

OIL PIPELINE

HELIUM NITROGEN

Medicine Hat

Swift Current

OIL PIPELINE Old Wives L.

CLAY

Milk R.

Weyburn

Souris R.

Estevan

UNITED STATES

A 116° B 114° C 112° D 110° E 108° F 106° G 104° H 102° J 100° K
60° 1 58° 2 56° 3 54° 4 52° 5 50° 6

B 114° C 112° D 110° E 108° F 106° G 104° H 102° J

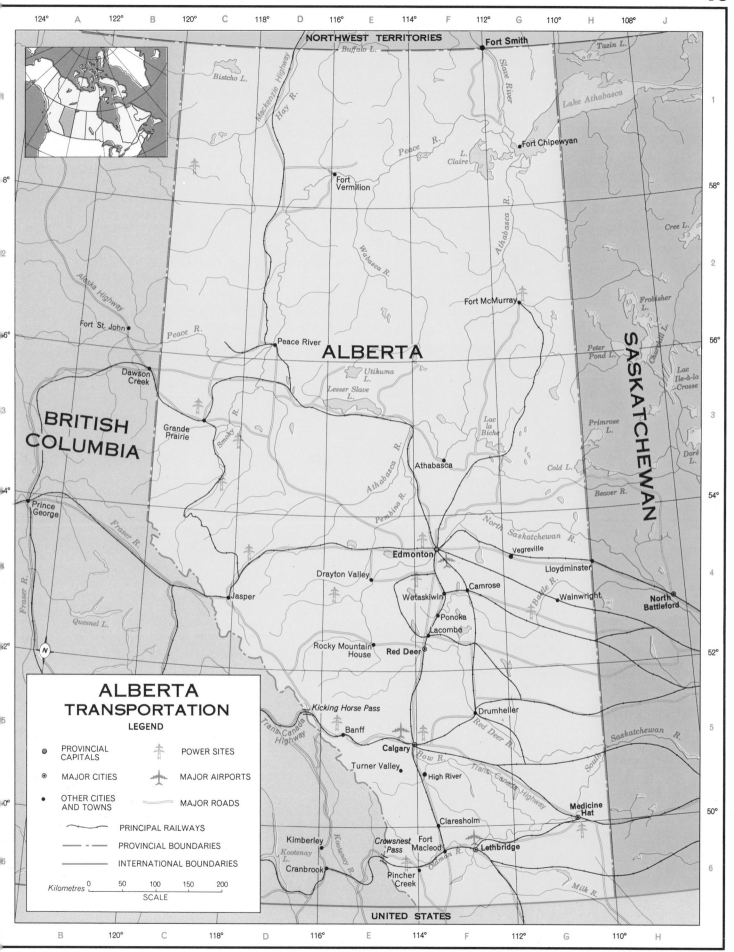

ALBERTA

BRITISH
COLUMBIA

SASKATCHEWAN

NORTHWEST TERRITORIES

UNITED STATES

ALBERTA
TRANSPORTATION
LEGEND

- PROVINCIAL CAPITALS
- MAJOR CITIES
- OTHER CITIES AND TOWNS
- POWER SITES
- MAJOR AIRPORTS
- MAJOR ROADS
- PRINCIPAL RAILWAYS
- PROVINCIAL BOUNDARIES
- INTERNATIONAL BOUNDARIES

Kilometres 0 50 100 150 200
SCALE

Fort Smith
Fort Chipewyan
Fort Vermilion
Fort McMurray
Fort St. John
Peace River
Dawson Creek
Grande Prairie
Athabasca
Prince George
Jasper
Drayton Valley
Edmonton
Vegreville
Lloydminster
Camrose
Wetaskiwin
Wainwright
North Battleford
Ponoka
Lacombe
Rocky Mountain House
Red Deer
Drumheller
Kicking Horse Pass
Banff
Calgary
Turner Valley
High River
Medicine Hat
Claresholm
Kimberley
Crowsnest Pass
Fort Macleod
Lethbridge
Cranbrook
Pincher Creek

Buffalo L.
Tazin L.
Bistcho L.
Lake Athabasca
Cree L.
Mackenzie Highway
Hay R.
Peace R.
Slave River
L. Claire
Webasca R.
Athabasca R.
Frobisher L.
Alaska Highway
Peace R.
Utikuma L.
Lesser Slave L.
Peter Pond L.
Lac Ile-à-la-Crosse
Smoky R.
Lac la Biche
Primrose L.
Doré L.
Athabasca R.
Cold L.
Pembina R.
Beaver R.
Fraser R.
North Saskatchewan R.
Battle R.
Quesnel L.
Red Deer R.
Saskatchewan R.
Trans-Canada Highway
Bow R.
Trans-Canada Highway
South Saskatchewan R.
Kootenay L.
Kootenay R.
Oldman R.
Milk R.
Fraser R.

124° 122° 120° 118° 116° 114° 112° 110° 108°
A B C D E F G H J

60° 58° 56° 54° 52° 50°
1 2 3 4 5 6

N

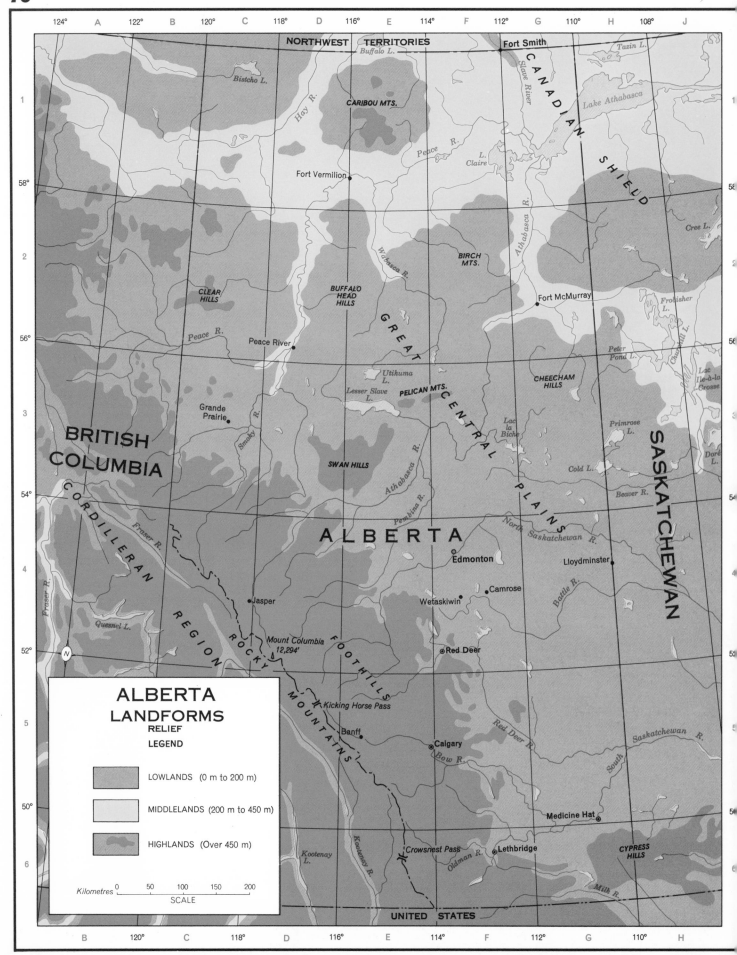

NORTHWEST TERRITORIES

Fort Smith

CANADIAN SHIELD

Buffalo L.

Bistcho L.

CARIBOU MTS.

Hay R.

Peace R.

Lake Athabasca

Tazin L.

Slave River

L. Claire

Cree L.

Fort Vermilion

Wabasca R.

BIRCH MTS.

Athabasca R.

Frobisher L.

CLEAR HILLS

BUFFALO HEAD HILLS

Fort McMurray

Peace R.

Peace River

GREAT

Utikuma L.

CHEECHAM HILLS

Peter Pond L.

Churchill L.

Lac Ile-à-la-Crosse

Lesser Slave L.

PELICAN MTS.

Grande Prairie

Smoky R.

Lac la Biche

Primrose L.

Doré L.

BRITISH COLUMBIA

CENTRAL

SWAN HILLS

Athabasca R.

Cold L.

SASKATCHEWAN

Fraser R.

CORDILLERAN

Pembina R.

North Saskatchewan R.

Beaver R.

PLAINS

ALBERTA

Edmonton

Lloydminster

REGION

Camrose

Battle R.

Quesnel L.

Wetaskiwin

Jasper

FOOTHILLS

Mount Columbia 12,294'

Red Deer

ROCKY

Kicking Horse Pass

Red Deer R.

Saskatchewan R.

Banff

Calgary

MOUNTAINS

Bow R.

South Saskatchewan R.

ALBERTA
LANDFORMS
RELIEF
LEGEND

LOWLANDS (0 m to 200 m)

MIDDLELANDS (200 m to 450 m)

HIGHLANDS (Over 450 m)

Medicine Hat

CYPRESS HILLS

Kootenay L.

Kootenay R.

Crowsnest Pass

Lethbridge

Oldman R.

Kilometres   0   50   100   150   200
SCALE

Milk R.

UNITED STATES

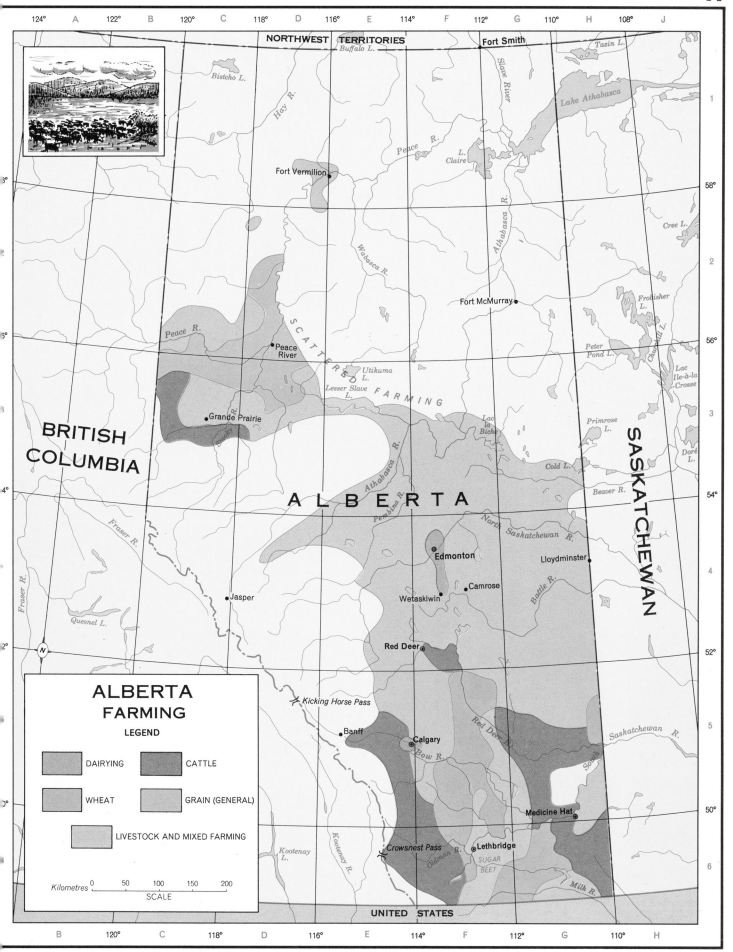

| | 124° | A | 122° | B | 120° | C | 118° | D | 116° | E | 114° | F | 112° | G | 110° | H | 108° | J |

NORTHWEST TERRITORIES

Fort Smith

Buffalo L.

Bistcho L.

Tazin L.

Hay R.

Lake Athabasca

Peace R.

Fort Vermilion

L. Claire

58°

Athabasca R.

Cree L.

Wabasca R.

Fort McMurray

Frobisher L.

56°

S C A T T E R E D

Peace River

Peter Pond L.

Lac Ile-à-la-Crosse

Peace R.

Utikuma L.

F A R M I N G

Lesser Slave L.

Grande Prairie

Smoky R.

Lac la Biche

Primrose L.

Doré L.

BRITISH
COLUMBIA

A L B E R T A

Cold L.

Athabasca R.

Beaver R.

54°

Fraser R.

Pembina R.

North Saskatchewan R.

SASKATCHEWAN

Jasper

Edmonton

Lloydminster

Quesnel L.

Camrose

Wetaskiwin

Battle R.

Fraser R.

N

Red Deer

52°

Kicking Horse Pass

Saskatchewan R.

Banff

Red Deer R.

Calgary

Bow R.

South Saskatchewan R.

**ALBERTA
FARMING**

LEGEND

Medicine Hat

50°

DAIRYING   CATTLE

Crowsnest Pass

Oldman R.

Lethbridge

WHEAT   GRAIN (GENERAL)

SUGAR BEET

LIVESTOCK AND MIXED FARMING

Kootenay L.

Kootenay R.

Milk R.

Kilometres 0   50   100   150   200
SCALE

UNITED STATES

| | B | 120° | C | 118° | D | 116° | E | 114° | F | 112° | G | 110° | H |

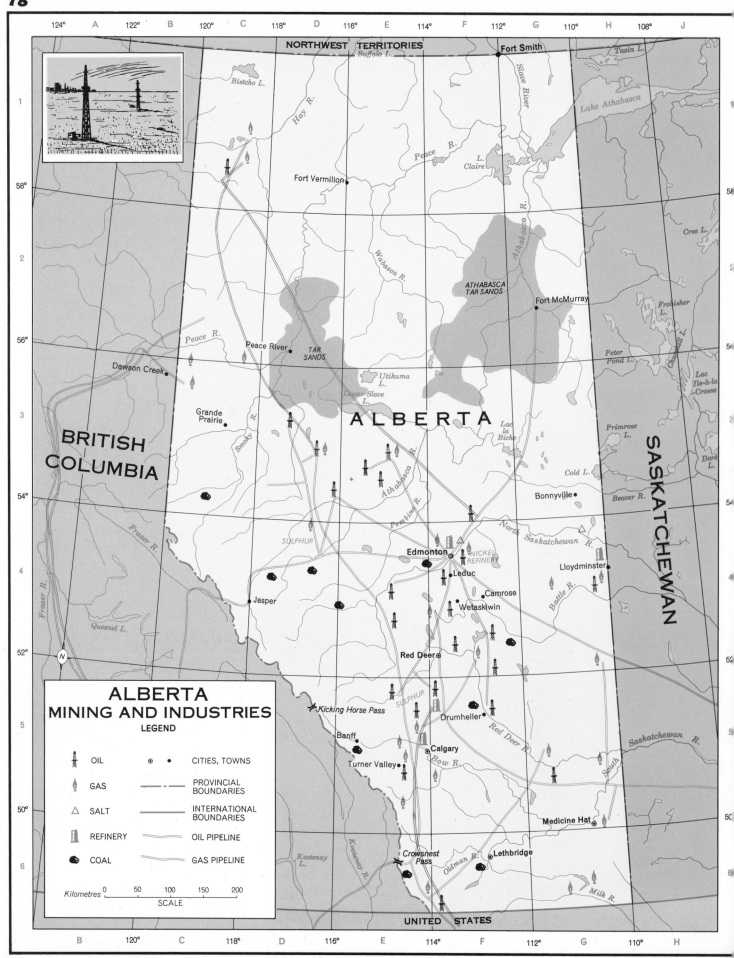

NORTHWEST TERRITORIES
Fort Smith

BRITISH COLUMBIA

A L B E R T A

ATHABASCA TAR SANDS

Fort McMurray

SASKATCHEWAN

Lake Athabasca

Bistcho L.

Buffalo L.

Hay R.

Peace R.

L. Claire

Slave River

Tazin L.

Cree L.

Frobisher L.

Peter Pond L.

Lac Ile-à-la-Crosse

Doré L.

Fort Vermilion

Wabasca R.

Athabasca R.

Utikuma L.

Lesser Slave L.

Peace R.

Peace River

TAR SANDS

Dawson Creek

Grande Prairie

Smoky R.

Lac la Biche

Primrose L.

Cold L.

Bonnyville

Beaver R.

Fraser R.

Athabasca R.

Pembina R.

SULPHUR

North Saskatchewan R.

Battle R.

Lloydminster

Jasper

Edmonton
NICKEL REFINERY
Leduc
Camrose
Wetaskiwin

Quesnel L.

Red Deer

Kicking Horse Pass

SULPHUR

Drumheller

Red Deer R.

Saskatchewan R.

Banff

Turner Valley

Calgary

Bow R.

South Saskatchewan R.

Medicine Hat

Kootenay L.

Kootenay R.

Crowsnest Pass

Oldman R.

Lethbridge

Milk R.

UNITED STATES

ALBERTA
MINING AND INDUSTRIES
LEGEND

OIL		CITIES, TOWNS	
GAS		PROVINCIAL BOUNDARIES	
SALT		INTERNATIONAL BOUNDARIES	
REFINERY		OIL PIPELINE	
COAL		GAS PIPELINE	

Kilometres   0   50   100   150   200
SCALE

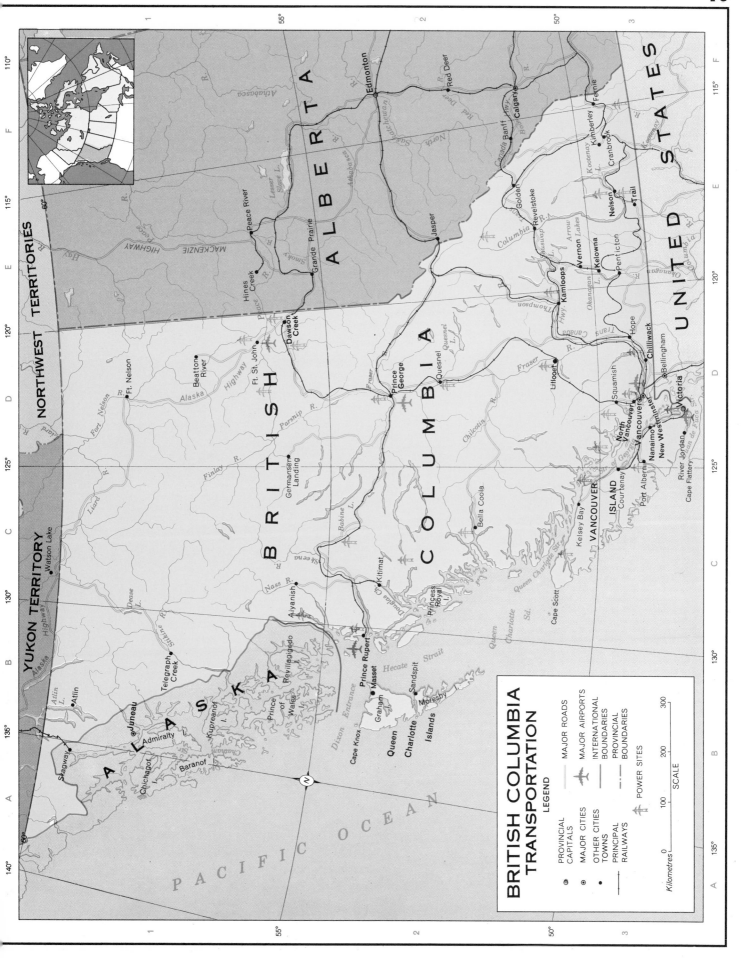

BRITISH COLUMBIA TRANSPORTATION

LEGEND

PROVINCIAL CAPITALS		MAJOR ROADS	
MAJOR CITIES		MAJOR AIRPORTS	
OTHER CITIES TOWNS		INTERNATIONAL BOUNDARIES	
PRINCIPAL RAILWAYS		PROVINCIAL BOUNDARIES	
		POWER SITES	

SCALE

Kilometres 0   100   200   300

NORTHWEST TERRITORIES

YUKON TERRITORY

ALASKA

ALBERTA

BRITISH COLUMBIA

UNITED STATES

PACIFIC OCEAN

Edmonton
Red Deer
Calgary
Banff
Canada
Fernie
Kimberley
Cranbrook
Nelson
Trail
Goldei
Revelstoke
Vernon
Kelowna
Penticton
Kamloops
Hope
Chilliwack
Bellingham
Victoria
Lillooet
Squamish
Vancouver
North Vancouver
New Westminster
Nanaimo
Port Alberni
Courtenay
VANCOUVER ISLAND
River Jordan
Cape Flattery

Jasper
Quesnel
Prince George
Bella Coola
Kelsey Bay
Cape Scott

Peace River
Grande Prairie
Hines Creek
Dawson Creek
Ft. St. John
Beatton River
Ft. Nelson

Watson Lake
Atlin
Telegraph Creek
Juneau
Admiralty
Skagway
Chichagof I.
Baranof I.
Kupreanof I.
Prince of Wales I.
Revillagigedo I.

Germansen Landing

Kitimat
Aiyanish
Prince Rupert
Masset
Graham I.
Sandspit
Moresby I.
Queen Charlotte Islands
Cape Knox

Princess Royal I.

Athabasca R.
Lesser Slave L.
Peace R.
Smoky R.
Saskatchewan R.
North Saskatchewan R.
Bow R.
Red Deer R.
Columbia R.
Arrow Lakes
Shuswap L.
Okanagan L.
Kootenay R.
Thompson R.
Fraser R.
Quesnel L.
Chilcotin R.
Parsnip R.
Finlay R.
Liard R.
Fort Nelson R.
Nass R.
Skeena R.
Babine L.
Stikine R.
Dease L.
Atlin L.
Hay R.
MACKENZIE HIGHWAY
Alaska Highway
Trans Canada Hwy.
Fraser R.
Douglas Ch.
Hecate Strait
Queen Charlotte Sd.
Queen Charlotte Strait
Strait of Georgia
Juan de Fuca Str.
Dixon Entrance
Cape Scott

N

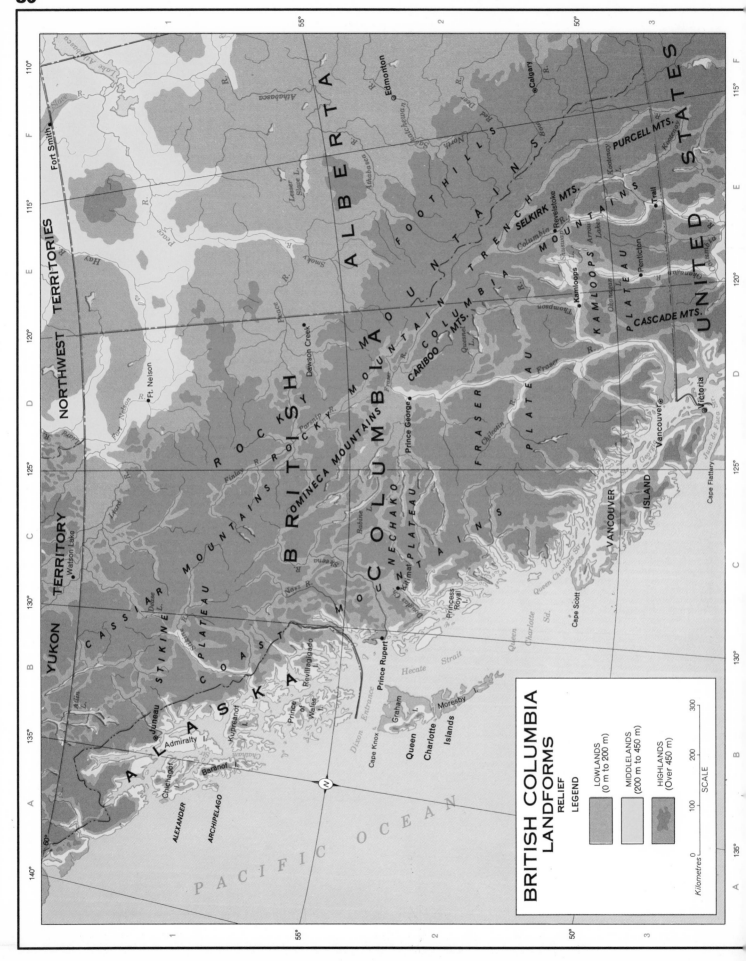

PACIFIC OCEAN

BRITISH COLUMBIA LANDFORMS

RELIEF
LEGEND

LOWLANDS
(0 m to 200 m)

MIDDLELANDS
(200 m to 450 m)

HIGHLANDS
(Over 450 m)

SCALE

Kilometres 0   100   200   300

NORTHWEST TERRITORIES

YUKON TERRITORY

ALBERTA

BRITISH COLUMBIA

UNITED STATES

ALASKA

ALEXANDER ARCHIPELAGO

Queen Charlotte Islands

Vancouver Island

Edmonton

Calgary

Fort Smith

Ft. Nelson

Dawson Creek

Watson Lake

Prince George

Prince Rupert

Kamloops

Penticton

Trail

Revelstoke

Vancouver

Victoria

Juneau

ROCKY MOUNTAINS

PURCELL MTS.

SELKIRK MTS.

FOOTHILLS

CASCADE MTS.

KAMLOOPS PLATEAU

FRASER PLATEAU

NECHAKO PLATEAU

CARIBOO MTS.

ROMINECA MOUNTAINS

CASSIAR MOUNTAINS

STIKINE PLATEAU

COAST MOUNTAINS

ROCKY MOUNTAIN TRENCH

COLUMBIA MOUNTAINS

Lake Athabasca

Slave R.

Peace R.

Athabasca R.

Hay R.

Liard R.

Finlay R.

Parsnip R.

Skeena R.

Fraser R.

Thompson R.

Columbia R.

Kootenay R.

Okanagan R.

Hecate Strait

Queen Charlotte Sound

Dixon Entrance

Cape Flattery

Cape Scott

Cape Knox

Graham I.

Moresby I.

Princess Royal I.

Revillagigedo I.

Prince of Wales I.

Baranof I.

Chichagof I.

Admiralty I.

Kupreanof I.

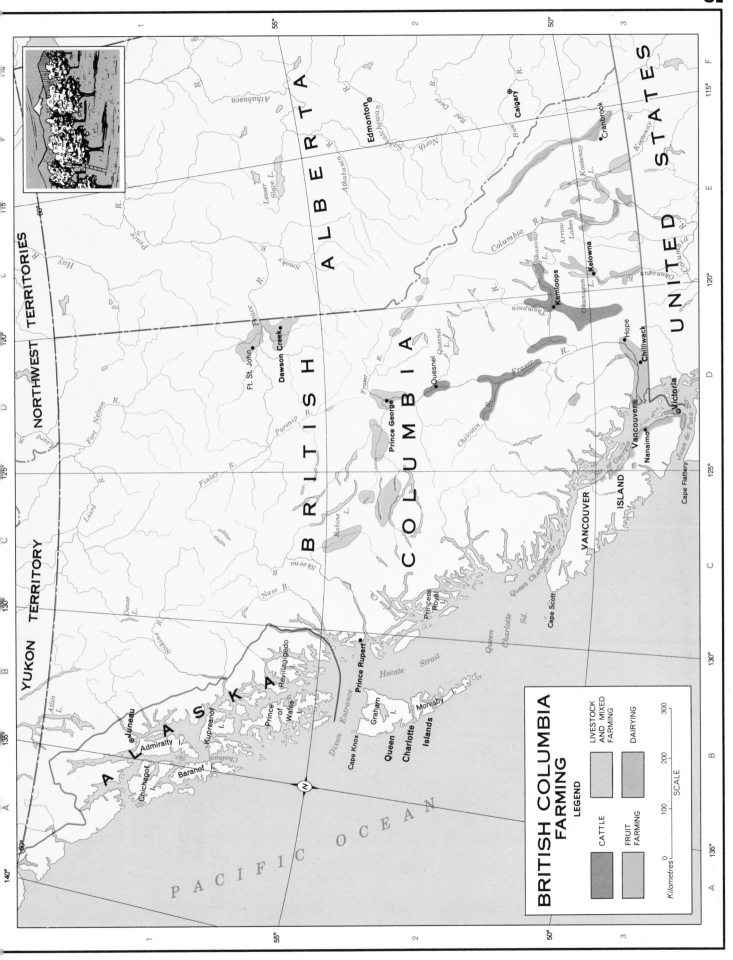

BRITISH COLUMBIA FARMING

LEGEND

CATTLE

FRUIT FARMING

LIVESTOCK AND MIXED FARMING

DAIRYING

SCALE

Kilometres 0   100   200   300

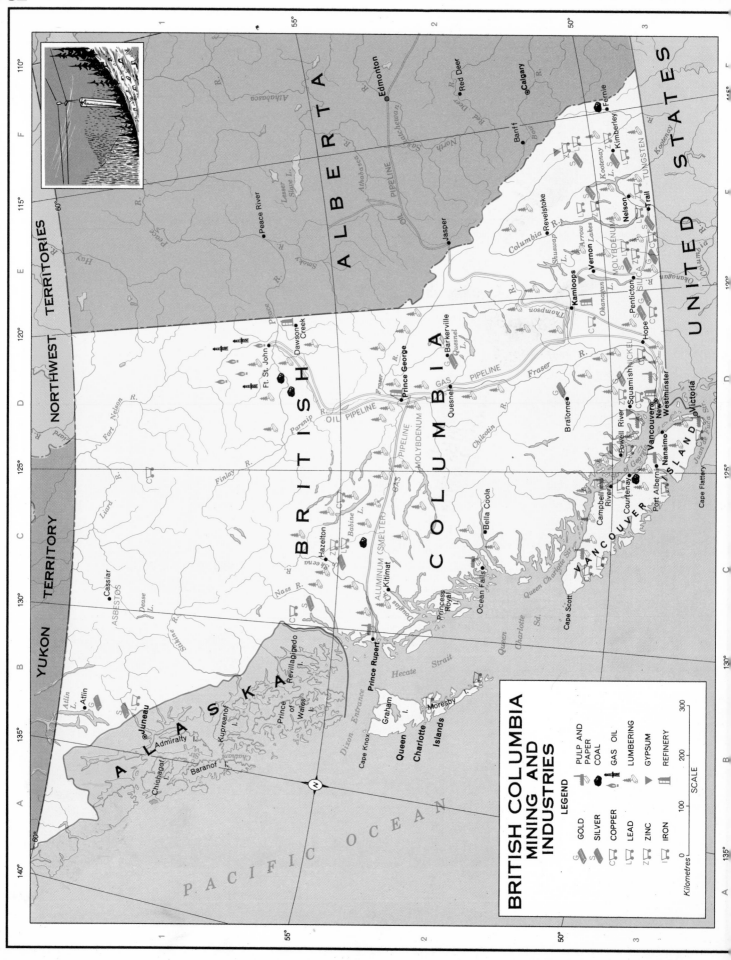

BRITISH COLUMBIA
MINING AND
INDUSTRIES

THE CANADIAN NORTHLAND

LEGEND

- ADMINISTRATIVE CAPITALS
- CITIES, TOWNS, VILLAGES
- OIL
- GAS
- OIL AND GAS RESERVES
- COAL

- GOLD
- SILVER — S
- NICKEL — N
- COPPER — C
- LEAD — L
- ZINC — Z

SCALE

Kilometres 0 200 400 600

GREENLAND (DENMARK)

ALASKA (U.S.)

QUEBEC

MANITOBA

SASKATCHEWAN

ALBERTA

BRITISH COLUMBIA

YUKON TERRITORY

NORTHWEST TERRITORIES

DISTRICT OF MACKENZIE

DISTRICT OF KEEWATIN

DISTRICT OF FRANKLIN

ELLESMERE ISLAND

QUEEN ELIZABETH ISLANDS

BAFFIN ISLAND

VICTORIA ISLAND

DISTRICT OF FRANKLIN

Prince Charles I.

HUDSON BAY

DAVIS STRAIT

Baffin Bay

Arctic Circle

BEAUFORT SEA

Amundsen Gulf

Coronation Gulf

Queen Maud Gulf

M'Clure Strait

Viscount Melville Sound

M'Clintock Channel

Prince Regent Inlet

Lancaster Sound

Boothia Peninsula

Gulf of Boothia

Melville Peninsula

Foxe Basin

Foxe Channel

Hudson Strait

Cumberland Sd.

Frobisher Bay

Welcome Sound

Banks Island

Prince Patrick I.

Melville Island

MacKenzie King I.

Ellef Ringnes I.

Axel Heiberg Island

Bathurst I.

Cornwallis I.

Devon Island

Somerset I.

Prince of Wales I.

King William I.

Southampton Island

Coats I.

Mansel I.

Ottawa Is.

Belcher Is.

Bylot I.

Broughton Is.

Resolute

Grise Fiord

Arctic Bay

Pond Inlet

Clyde

Cape Dyer

Pangnirtung

Frobisher (Iqaluit)

Lake Harbour

Cape Dorset

Hall Beach

Igloolik

Repulse Bay

Coral Harbour

Chesterfield Inlet

Baker Lake

Rankin Inlet

Whale Cove

Eskimo Point

Churchill

Cape Churchill

Spence Bay

Gjoa Haven

Pelly Bay

Cambridge Bay

Bathurst Inlet

Read Island

Holman

Sachs Harbour

Coppermine

Snowdrift

Reliance

Rae Lakes

Rae

Edzo

Yellowknife

Detah

Fort Resolution

Pine Point

Fort Smith

Fort Providence

Hay River

Enterprise

Trout Lake

Fort Nelson

Fort Liard

Nahanni Butte

Fort Simpson

Wrigley

Norman Wells

Fort Norman

Fort Franklin

Fort Good Hope

Colville Lake

Arctic Red River

Fort McPherson

Aklavik

Inuvik

Tuktoyaktuk

Paulatuk

Cape Bathurst

Old Crow

Fort Yukon

Fairbanks

Dawson

Mayo

Elsa

Keno Hill

Carmacks

Whitehorse

Haines Junction

Carcross

Teslin

Watson Lake

Skagway

Juneau

Uranium City

Churchill

Port Harrison

Sanikiluaq

Great Whale River

Fort Chimo

Povungnituk

Sugluk

Ungava Bay

Port Radium (Echo Bay)

Lac La Martre

Rocher River

Reliance

Great Bear Lake

Great Slave Lake

Lake Athabasca

Lac la Biche

Aberdeen L.

Back R.

Thelon R.

Dubawnt R.

Contwoyto L.

Nueltin L.

Mackenzie R.

Peel R.

Porcupine R.

Yukon River

Tanana R.

Pelly R.

Stewart R.

Liard R.

South Nahanni R.

Peace R.

Athabasca R.

Slave R.

Nelson R.

Churchill R.

Coppermine R.

Thomsen

Copper Permafrost

Southern Limit of Continuous Permafrost

Southern Limit of Discontinuous Permafrost

Tree Line

URANIUM

ASBESTOS

KLONDIKE

Pipeline

Highway

Prince Gustav Adolf Sea

Cape Stallworthy

Cape Columbia

Alert

Cape Dorchester

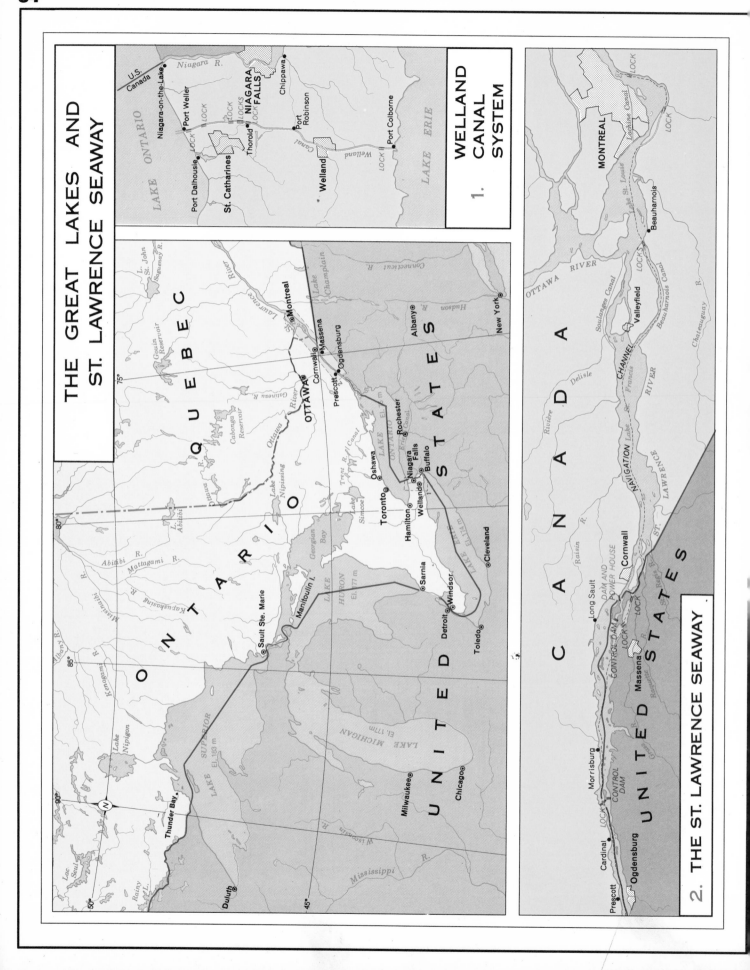

THE GREAT LAKES AND ST. LAWRENCE SEAWAY

1. WELLAND CANAL SYSTEM

2. THE ST. LAWRENCE SEAWAY

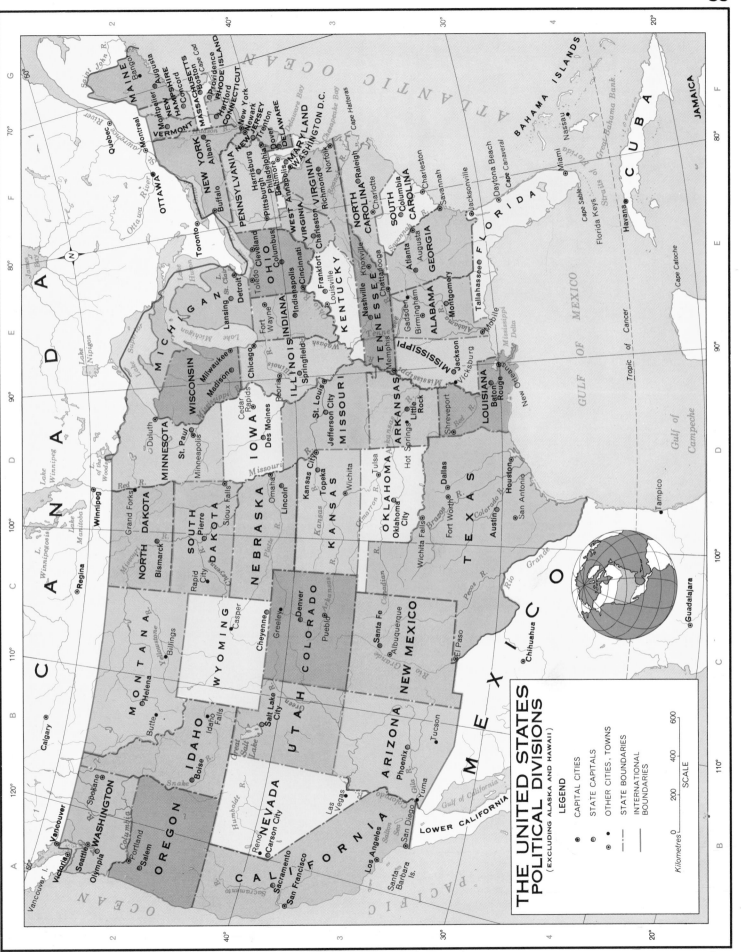

THE UNITED STATES
POLITICAL DIVISIONS
(EXCLUDING ALASKA AND HAWAII)

LEGEND

- ◉ CAPITAL CITIES
- ◉ STATE CAPITALS
- ◉ OTHER CITIES, TOWNS
- —·—·— STATE BOUNDARIES
- ——— INTERNATIONAL BOUNDARIES

SCALE

Kilometres 0 200 400 600

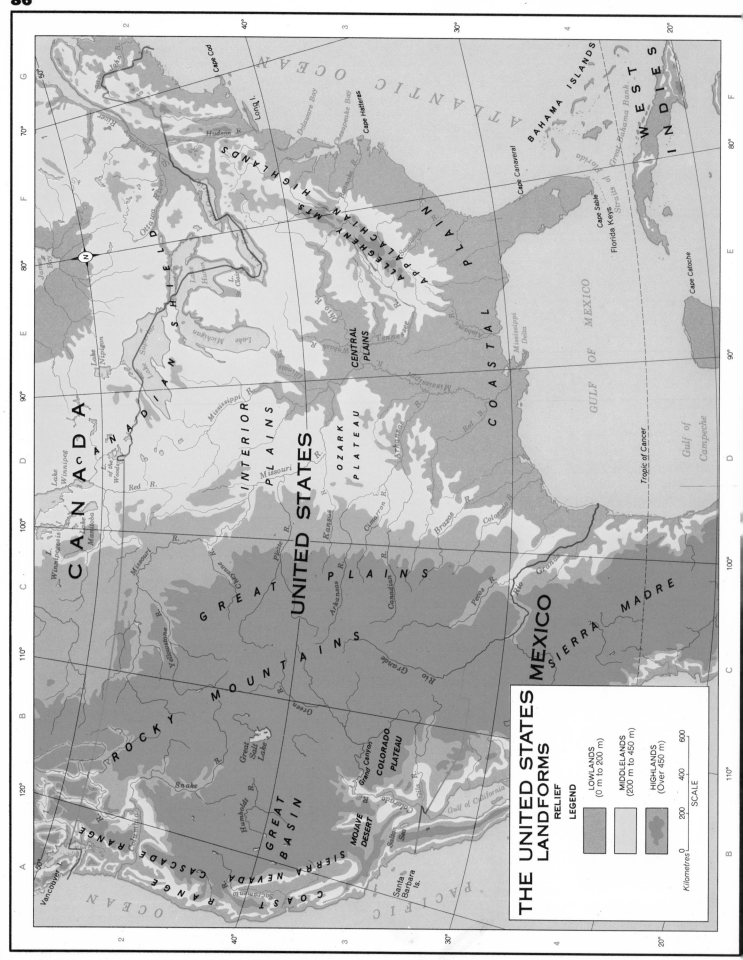

THE UNITED STATES
LANDFORMS

RELIEF

LEGEND

LOWLANDS
(0 to 200 m)

MIDDLELANDS
(200 m to 450 m)

HIGHLANDS
(Over 450 m)

SCALE

Kilometres   0   200   400   600

CANADA

UNITED STATES

MEXICO

WEST INDIES

ATLANTIC OCEAN

PACIFIC OCEAN

GULF OF MEXICO

Gulf of Campeche

CANADIAN SHIELD

ROCKY MOUNTAINS

GREAT PLAINS

INTERIOR PLAINS

CENTRAL PLAINS

COASTAL PLAIN

APPALACHIAN MTS

ALLEGHENY HIGHLANDS

OZARK PLATEAU

COLORADO PLATEAU

GREAT BASIN

MOJAVE DESERT

SIERRA NEVADA

CASCADE RANGE

COAST RANGE

SIERRA MADRE

Grand Canyon

Great Salt Lake

Gulf of California

Salton Sea

Santa Barbara Is.

Tropic of Cancer

Cape Catoche

Cape Sable

Cape Canaveral

Florida Keys

Straits of Florida

Great Bahama Bank

BAHAMA ISLANDS

Cape Hatteras

Chesapeake Bay

Delaware Bay

Long I.

Cape Cod

Cape Cod

Hudson R.

Ottawa River

St. Lawrence River

James Bay

Hudson Bay

Lake Winnipeg

Lake Manitoba

L. of the Woods

Lake Nipigon

Lake Superior

Lake Michigan

Lake Huron

L. St. Clair

Lake Erie

Ohio R.

Wabash R.

Tennessee R.

Savannah R.

Alabama R.

Mississippi Delta

Red R.

Arkansas R.

Missouri R.

Illinois R.

Mississippi R.

Platte R.

Kansas R.

Cimarron R.

Canadian R.

Brazos R.

Colorado R.

Pecos R.

Rio Grande

Red R.

Cheyenne R.

Yellowstone R.

Missouri R.

Green R.

Snake R.

Columbia R.

Sacramento R.

Humboldt R.

Gila R.

Colorado R.

Vancouver I.

Vancouver

St. John R.

Red R.

Winnipegosis

50°   40°   30°   20°

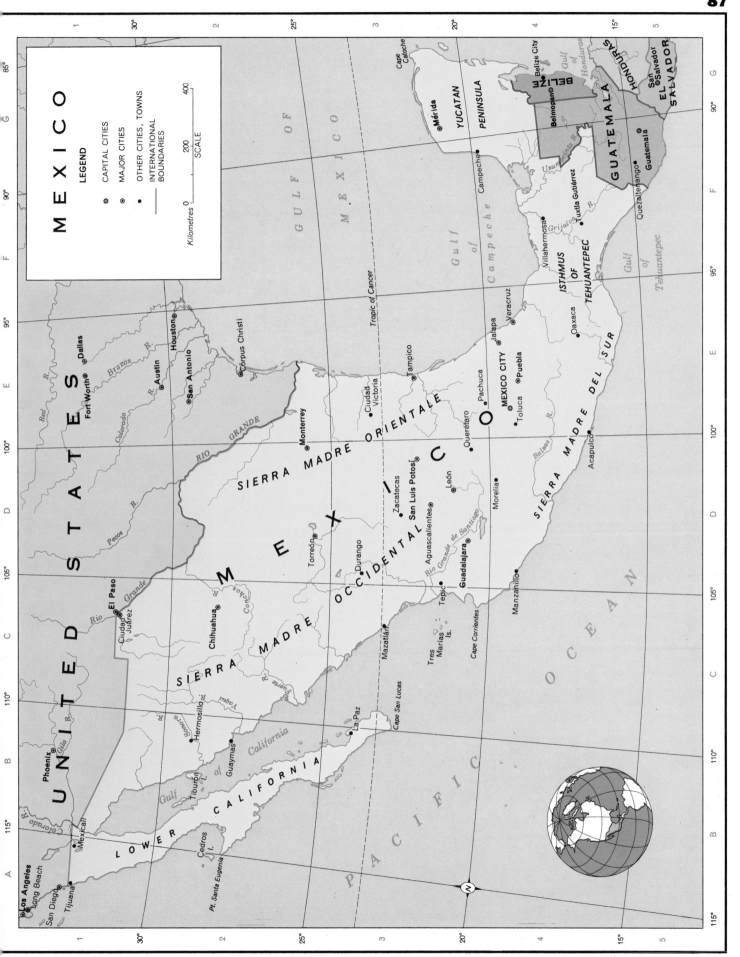

MEXICO

LEGEND

● CAPITAL CITIES
◉ MAJOR CITIES
• OTHER CITIES, TOWNS
— INTERNATIONAL BOUNDARIES

SCALE

Kilometres 0   200   400

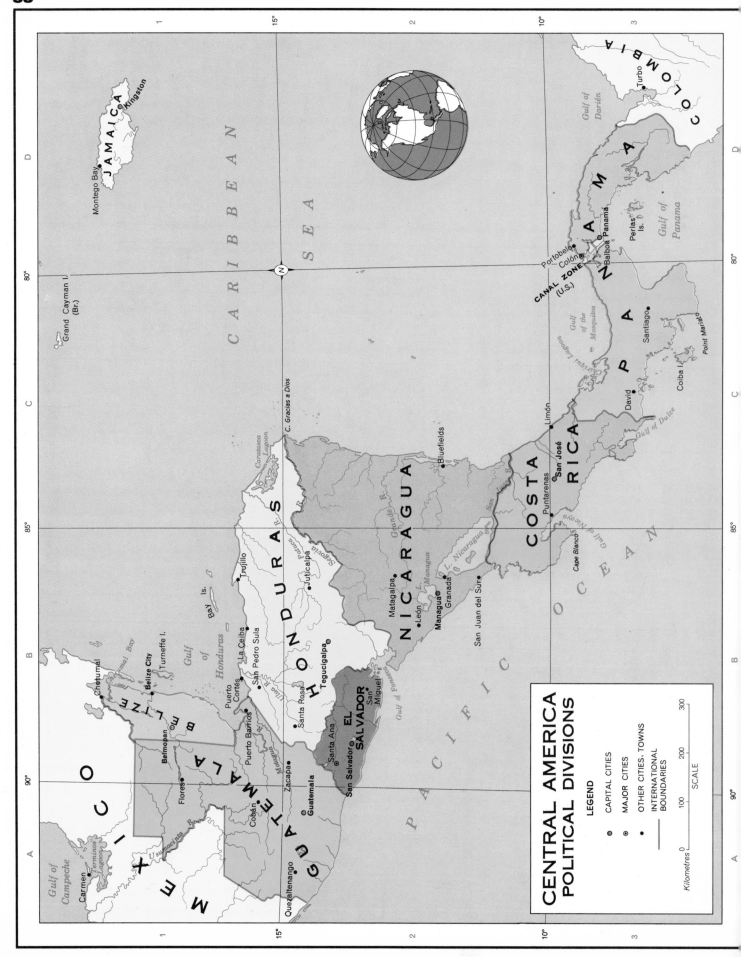

CENTRAL AMERICA
POLITICAL DIVISIONS

LEGEND

⊙ CAPITAL CITIES
◉ MAJOR CITIES
• OTHER CITIES, TOWNS
— INTERNATIONAL BOUNDARIES

SCALE

Kilometres 0 100 200 300

JAMAICA
Kingston
Montego Bay

Grand Cayman I.
(Br.)

CARIBBEAN SEA

COLOMBIA
Turbo

Gulf of Darién

PANAMA
Panamá
Balboa
Colón
Portobelo
CANAL ZONE (U.S.)

Perlas Is.
Gulf of Panama

Gulf of the Mosquitos

Santiago
David
Point Mariato
Coiba I.

Chiriquí Lagoon
Gulf of Dulce

COSTA RICA
Limón
San José
Puntarenas
Gulf of Nicoya
Cape Blanco

C. Gracias a Dios

Carataseca Lagoon

NICARAGUA
Bluefields
Matagalpa
Managua
L. Managua
León
Granada
L. Nicaragua
San Juan del Sur
R. San Juan
Grande R.
Segovia R.

HONDURAS
Trujillo
Juticalpa
La Ceiba
Tegucigalpa
San Pedro Sula
Bay Is.
Gulf of Honduras
Ulúa R.
Patuca R.

Belize City
Turneffe I.
Chetumal
Chetumal Bay

BELIZE
Belmopan
Puerto Cortés
Puerto Barrios
Santa Rosa
Zacapa
Motagua R.

GUATEMALA
Guatemala
Cobán
Flores
Quezaltenango
Usumacinta R.

EL SALVADOR
Santa Ana
San Salvador
San Miguel
Gulf of Fonseca

MEXICO
Gulf of Campeche
Carmen
Terminos Lagoon

PACIFIC OCEAN

N

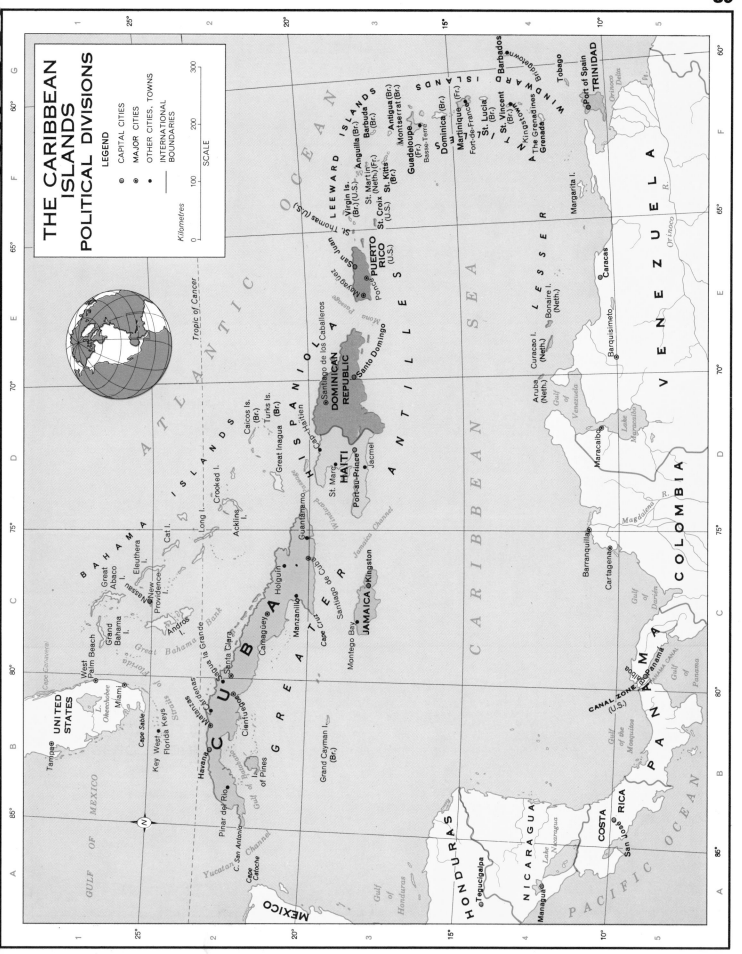

SOUTH AMERICA
POLITICAL DIVISIONS

LEGEND

- ⊙ CAPITAL CITIES
- ⊙ MAJOR CITIES
- • OTHER CITIES, TOWNS
- — INTERNATIONAL BOUNDARIES

Kilometres 0   400   800   1200
SCALE

SOUTH AMERICA
LANDFORMS
RELIEF
LEGEND
LOWLANDS (0 m to 200 m)
MIDDLELANDS (200 m to 450 m)
HIGHLANDS (Over 450 m)
Kilometres 0 400 800 1200
SCALE
CARIBBEAN SEA
Cape Gallinas
Gulf of Venezuela
Gulf of Darién
TRINIDAD
Orinoco Delta
LLANOS
Orinoco R.
Gulf of Panama
Magdalena R.
GUIANA HIGHLANDS
Essequibo R.
Equator
Negro R.
AMAZON R.
Amazon R.
SELVAS
Cape São Roque
Cape Aguja
Marañón R.
Ucayali R.
Madeira R.
Xingú R.
Tocantins R.
São Francisco R.
MATO GROSSO UPLAND
ANDES
L. Titicaca
PLATEAU OF BOLIVIA
Tropic of Capricorn
Paraguay R.
Paraná R.
GRAN CHACO
BRAZILIAN HIGHLANDS
Cape Frio
CAMPOS
Uruguay R.
PACIFIC OCEAN
ATLANTIC OCEAN
Río de la Plata
PAMPAS
Colorado R.
PATAGONIA
Chiloé I.
CHONOS ARCHIPELAGO
Chico R.
Falkland Islands (Br.)
Strait of Magellan
Tierra del Fuego
Cape Horn

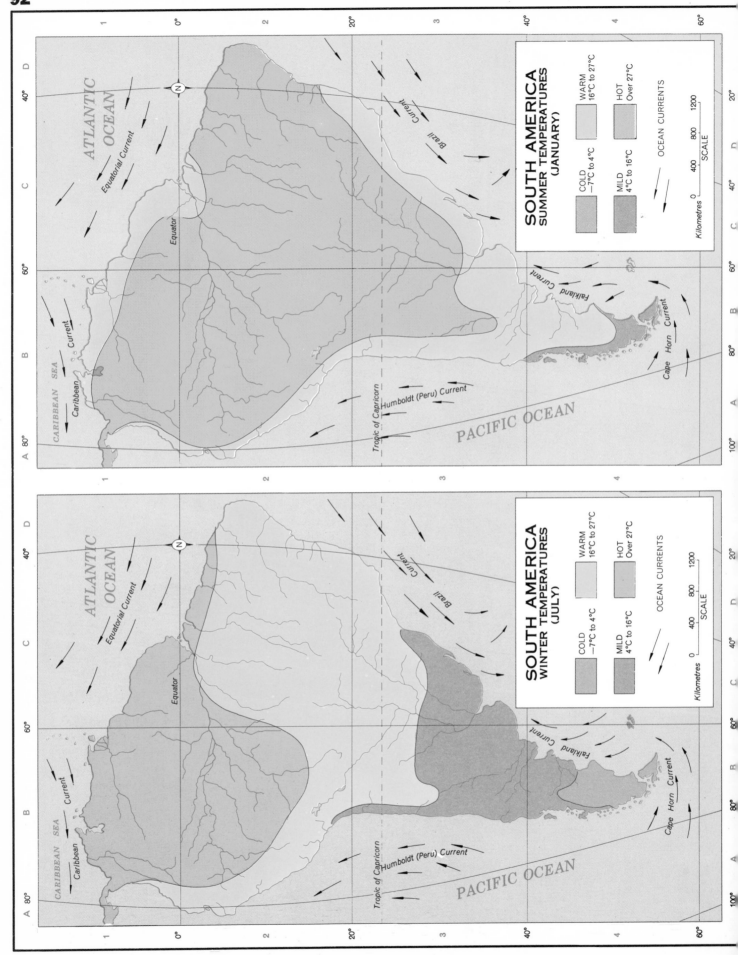

SOUTH AMERICA
SUMMER TEMPERATURES
(JANUARY)

COLD
−7°C to 4°C

MILD
4°C to 16°C

WARM
16°C to 27°C

HOT
Over 27°C

OCEAN CURRENTS

SCALE
Kilometres
0   400   800   1200

ATLANTIC OCEAN

Equatorial Current

Equator

CARIBBEAN SEA
Caribbean Current

Tropic of Capricorn

Humboldt (Peru) Current

PACIFIC OCEAN

Brazil Current

Falkland Current

Cape Horn Current

SOUTH AMERICA
WINTER TEMPERATURES
(JULY)

COLD
−7°C to 4°C

MILD
4°C to 16°C

WARM
16°C to 27°C

HOT
Over 27°C

OCEAN CURRENTS

SCALE
Kilometres
0   400   800   1200

ATLANTIC OCEAN

Equatorial Current

Equator

CARIBBEAN SEA
Caribbean Current

Tropic of Capricorn

Humboldt (Peru) Current

PACIFIC OCEAN

Brazil Current

Falkland Current

Cape Horn Current

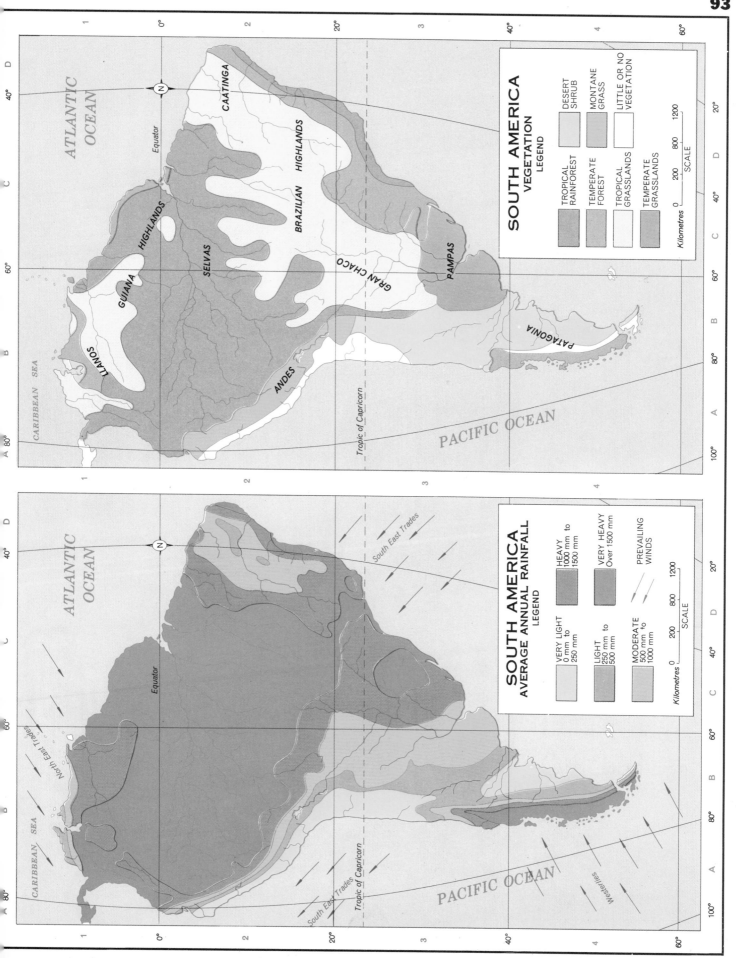

SOUTH AMERICA
VEGETATION
LEGEND

TROPICAL RAINFOREST	DESERT SHRUB
TEMPERATE FOREST	MONTANE GRASS
TROPICAL GRASSLANDS	LITTLE OR NO VEGETATION
TEMPERATE GRASSLANDS	

SCALE
Kilometres 0   200   400   800   1200

ATLANTIC OCEAN

PACIFIC OCEAN

CARIBBEAN SEA

Equator

Tropic of Capricorn

N

CAATINGA
BRAZILIAN HIGHLANDS
GUIANA HIGHLANDS
LLANOS
SELVAS
GRAN CHACO
ANDES
PAMPAS
PATAGONIA

SOUTH AMERICA
AVERAGE ANNUAL RAINFALL
LEGEND

VERY LIGHT 0 mm to 250 mm	HEAVY 1000 mm to 1500 mm
LIGHT 250 mm to 500 mm	VERY HEAVY Over 1500 mm
MODERATE 500 mm to 1000 mm	PREVAILING WINDS

SCALE
Kilometres 0   200   400   800   1200

ATLANTIC OCEAN

PACIFIC OCEAN

CARIBBEAN SEA

Equator

Tropic of Capricorn

N

North East Trades
South East Trades
South East Trades
Westerlies

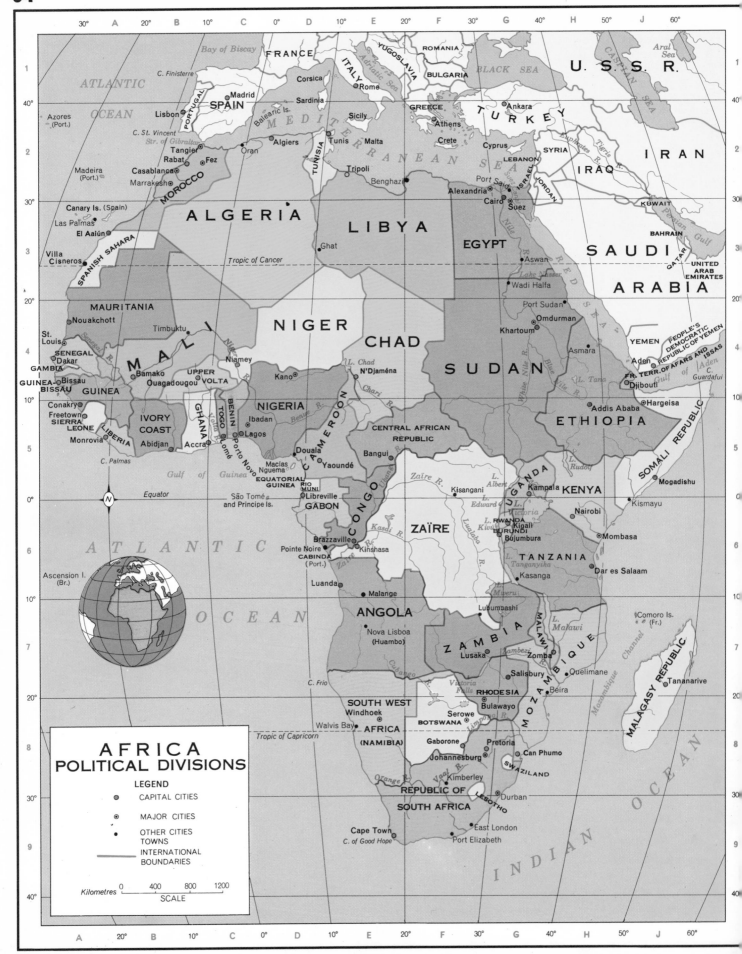

AFRICA
POLITICAL DIVISIONS

LEGEND

- ⦿ CAPITAL CITIES
- ⊙ MAJOR CITIES
- • OTHER CITIES TOWNS
- — INTERNATIONAL BOUNDARIES

Kilometres 0 400 800 1200
SCALE

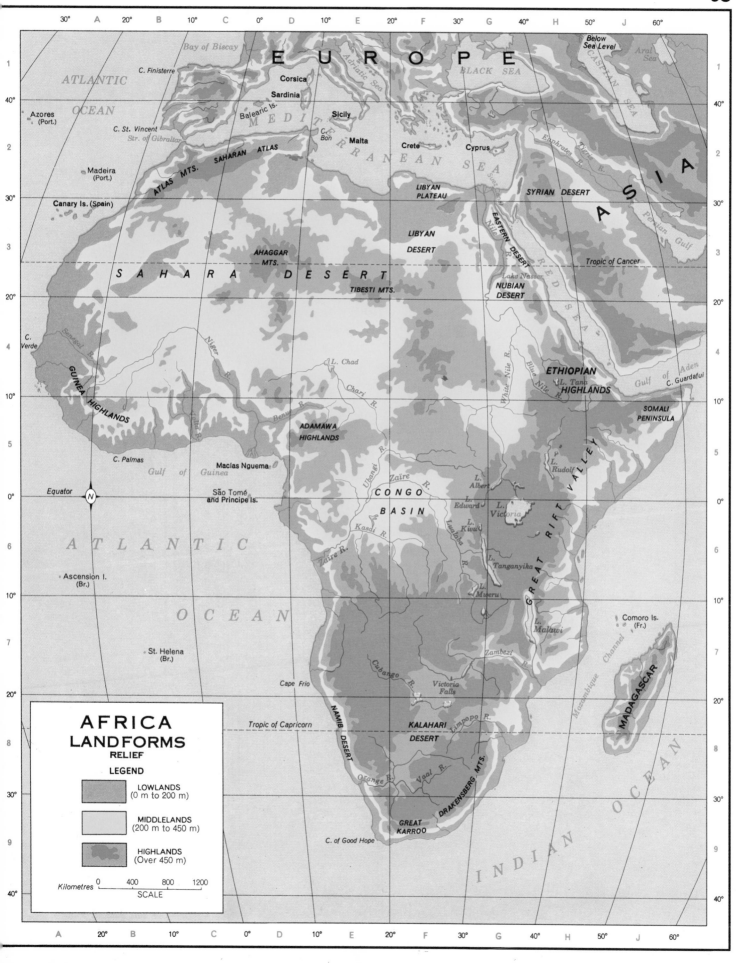

AFRICA
LANDFORMS
RELIEF

LEGEND

	LOWLANDS (0 m to 200 m)
	MIDDLELANDS (200 m to 450 m)
	HIGHLANDS (Over 450 m)

Kilometres 0   400   800   1200
SCALE

EUROPE

ASIA

ATLANTIC OCEAN

Azores (Port.)

Madeira (Port.)

Canary Is. (Spain)

C. Finisterre

C. St. Vincent

Str. of Gibraltar

Bay of Biscay

Corsica

Sardinia

Balearic Is.

Sicily

C. Bon

Malta

Crete

Cyprus

MEDITERRANEAN SEA

BLACK SEA

CASPIAN SEA

Aral Sea

Below Sea Level

Euphrates R.

Tigris R.

Persian Gulf

SYRIAN DESERT

LIBYAN PLATEAU

LIBYAN DESERT

EASTERN DESERT

Nile R.

Lake Nasser

NUBIAN DESERT

RED SEA

ATLAS MTS.

SAHARAN ATLAS

SAHARA DESERT

AHAGGAR MTS.

TIBESTI MTS.

Tropic of Cancer

C. Verde

Senegal R.

Niger R.

L. Chad

Chari R.

Volta R.

Benue R.

GUINEA HIGHLANDS

C. Palmas

Gulf of Guinea

Macías Nguema

São Tomé and Principe Is.

ADAMAWA HIGHLANDS

White Nile R.

Blue Nile R.

L. Tana

ETHIOPIAN HIGHLANDS

Gulf of Aden

C. Guardafui

SOMALI PENINSULA

Equator

N

ATLANTIC OCEAN

Ascension I. (Br.)

St. Helena (Br.)

Ubangi R.

Zaïre R.

CONGO BASIN

Kasai R.

Zaïre R.

Lualaba R.

L. Albert

L. Edward

L. Kivu

L. Victoria

L. Tanganyika

L. Mweru

L. Rudolf

GREAT RIFT VALLEY

L. Malawi

Cape Frio

Cubango R.

Victoria Falls

Zambezi R.

Limpopo R.

Mozambique Channel

Comoro Is. (Fr.)

MADAGASCAR

Tropic of Capricorn

NAMIB DESERT

KALAHARI DESERT

Orange R.

Vaal R.

DRAKENSBERG MTS.

GREAT KARROO

C. of Good Hope

INDIAN OCEAN

96

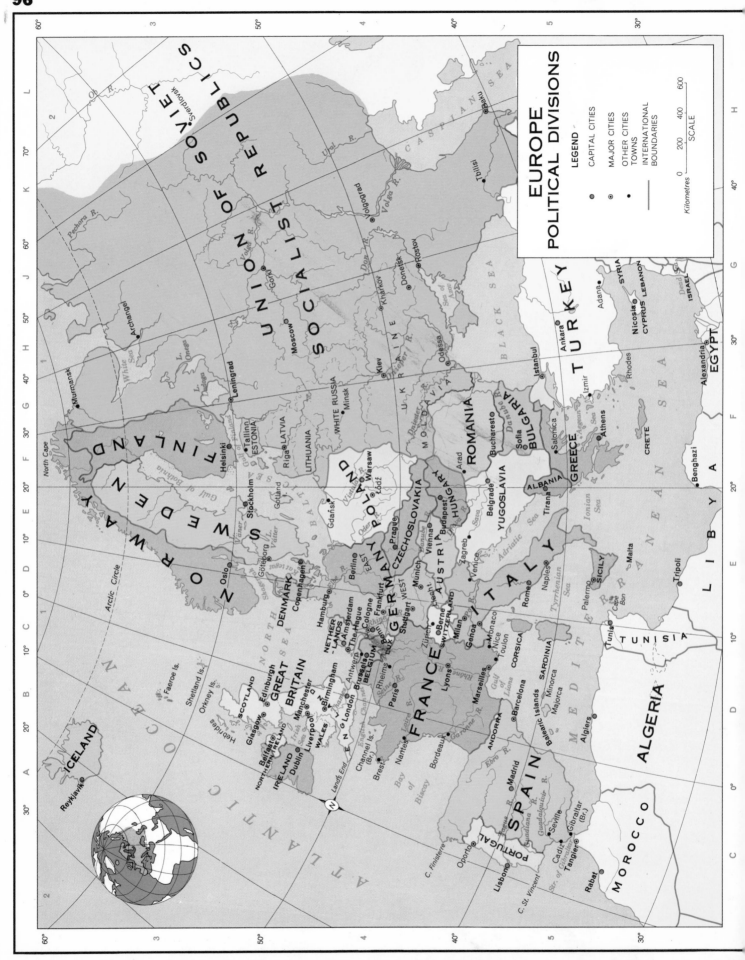

EUROPE
POLITICAL DIVISIONS

LEGEND

CAPITAL CITIES

MAJOR CITIES

OTHER CITIES

TOWNS

INTERNATIONAL
BOUNDARIES

SCALE

0   200   400   600

Kilometres

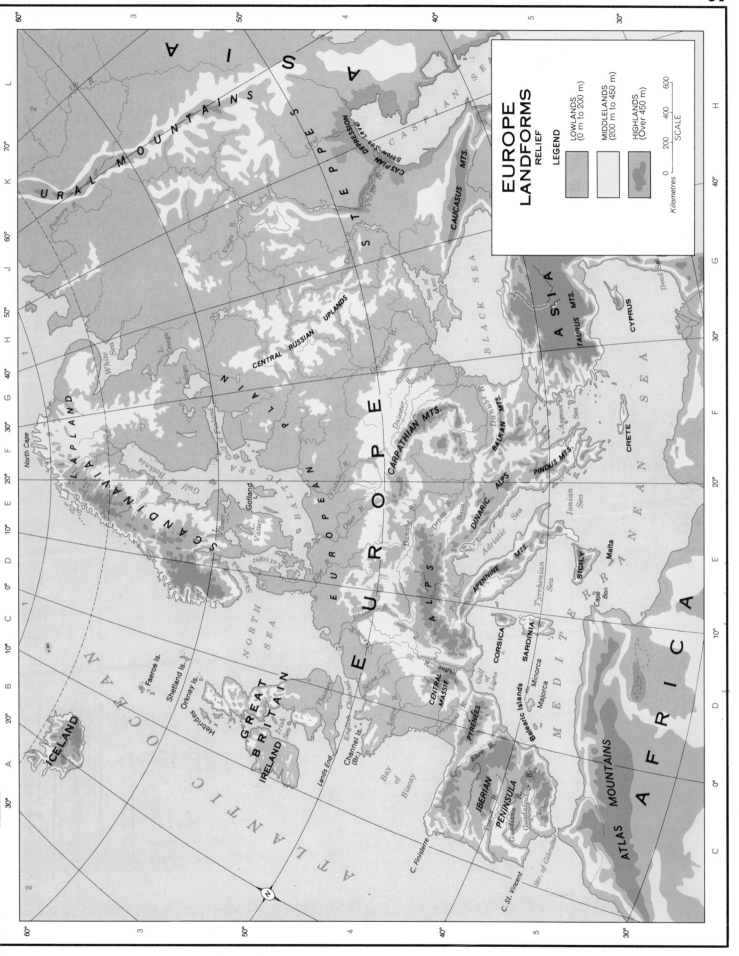

EUROPE LANDFORMS
RELIEF

LEGEND

LOWLANDS (0 m to 200 m)

MIDDLELANDS (200 m to 450 m)

HIGHLANDS (Over 450 m)

SCALE

Kilometres

0 200 400 600

A S I A

A F R I C A

URAL MOUNTAINS

Ob R.

Pechora R.

SCANDINAVIA

LAPLAND

ICELAND

ATLANTIC OCEAN

Faeroe Is.

Shetland Is.

Orkney Is.

Hebrides

GREAT BRITAIN

IRELAND

Irish Sea

Lands End

English Channel

Channel Is. (Br.)

Bay of Biscay

C. Finisterre

C. St. Vincent

Str. of Gibraltar

IBERIAN PENINSULA

Guadiana R.

Tagus R.

Ebro R.

Guadalquivir R.

PYRÉNÉES

Garonne R.

Loire R.

Seine R.

Thames R.

NORTH SEA

BALTIC SEA

Gulf of Bothnia

Gulf of Finland

White Sea

North Cape

L. Onega

L. Ladoga

Vychegda R.

Volga R.

P L A I N

CENTRAL RUSSIAN UPLANDS

E U R O P E A N

Dnieper R.

Dniester R.

CARPATHIAN MTS.

Don R.

Sea of Azov

BLACK SEA

CAUCASUS MTS.

CASPIAN SEA

CASPIAN DEPRESSION (Below Sea Level)

Ural R.

Volga R.

S T E P P E

TAURUS MTS.

CYPRUS

Dead Sea

MEDITERRANEAN SEA

Aegean Sea

CRETE

PINDUS MTS.

BALKAN MTS.

Danube R.

DINARIC ALPS

Adriatic Sea

Ionian Sea

Tyrrhenian Sea

APENNINE MTS.

SICILY

Malta

SARDINIA

CORSICA

Gulf of Lions

Balearic Islands

Minorca

Majorca

C. Bon

ATLAS MOUNTAINS

A L P S

CENTRAL MASSIF

Rhône R.

Rhine R.

Elbe R.

Oder R.

Weser R.

Vistula R.

Po R.

Sava R.

Drava R.

L. Vänern

L. Vättern

Gotland

Kattegat

Skagerrak

Göta R.

Oka R.

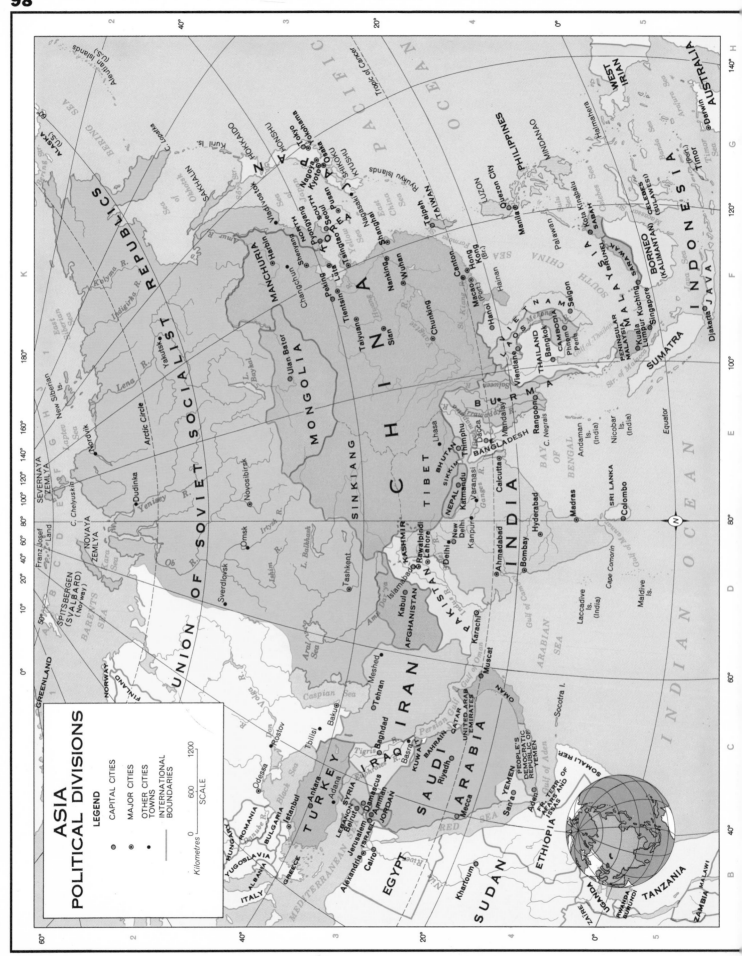

98

ASIA
POLITICAL DIVISIONS

LEGEND

● CAPITAL CITIES
◉ MAJOR CITIES
• OTHER CITIES
  TOWNS
— INTERNATIONAL
  BOUNDARIES

0   600   1200
Kilometres   SCALE

UNION OF SOVIET SOCIALIST REPUBLICS

CHINA

INDIA

MONGOLIA

SINKIANG

TIBET

MANCHURIA

JAPAN

KOREA

NORTH

SOUTH

VIETNAM

LAOS

THAILAND

BURMA

CAMBODIA

MALAYSIA

INDONESIA

BORNEO (KALIMANTAN)

SUMATRA

JAVA

CELEBES (SULAWESI)

PHILIPPINES

AUSTRALIA

WEST IRIAN

PAKISTAN

AFGHANISTAN

IRAN

IRAQ

TURKEY

SAUDI ARABIA

SYRIA

JORDAN

ISRAEL

LEBANON

KUWAIT

QATAR

UNITED ARAB EMIRATES

OMAN

YEMEN

PEOPLE'S DEMOCRATIC REPUBLIC OF YEMEN

BAHRAIN

EGYPT

SUDAN

ETHIOPIA

SOMALI REP.

TANZANIA

UGANDA

KENYA

RWANDA

BURUNDI

ZAIRE

ZAMBIA

MALAWI

NEPAL

BHUTAN

SIKKIM

BANGLADESH

SRI LANKA

KASHMIR

GREECE

ALBANIA

YUGOSLAVIA

BULGARIA

ROMANIA

HUNGARY

ITALY

NORWAY

FINLAND

GREENLAND

SPITSBERGEN (SVALBARD) (Norway)

NOVAYA ZEMLYA

SEVERNAYA ZEMLYA

Tokyo
Yokohama
Nagoya
Kyoto
Osaka
Pusan
Seoul
Pyongyang
Shenyang
Changchun
Harbin
Vladivostok
Peking
Tientsin
Tsingtao
Luta
Shanghai
Nanking
Wuhan
Taiyuan
Sian
Chunking
Canton
Hong Kong (Br.)
Macao (Port.)
Hanoi
Vientiane
Bangkok
Phnom Penh
Saigon
Rangoon
Mandalay
Kuala Lumpur
Singapore
Kuching
Kota Kinabalu
Manila
Quezon City
Djakarta
Darwin
Taipeh
Lhasa
Thimphu
Katmandu
Dacca
Calcutta
Varanasi
Kanpur
New Delhi
Delhi
Lahore
Rawalpindi
Islamabad
Ahmadabad
Bombay
Hyderabad
Madras
Colombo
Karachi
Kabul
Meshed
Tehran
Baghdad
Basra
Kuwait
Riyadh
Mecca
Sana
Aden
Muscat
Baku
Tbilisi
Ankara
Istanbul
Adana
Damascus
Beirut
Jerusalem
Amman
Cairo
Alexandria
Khartoum
Ulan Bator
Yakutsk
Nordvik
Dudinka
Novosibirsk
Omsk
Sverdlovsk
Tashkent
Rostov
Odessa
Kopetka

ARCTIC OCEAN

PACIFIC OCEAN

INDIAN OCEAN

ARABIAN SEA

BAY OF BENGAL

SOUTH CHINA SEA

EAST CHINA SEA

YELLOW SEA

SEA OF JAPAN

BERING SEA

KARA SEA

LAPTEV SEA

BARENTS SEA

EAST SIBERIAN SEA

CASPIAN SEA

BLACK SEA

RED SEA

MEDITERRANEAN SEA

ARAL SEA

L. Baikal

L. Balkhash

Tropic of Cancer

Arctic Circle

Equator

ALEUTIAN ISLANDS (U.S.)

ALASKA (U.S.)

HOKKAIDO

HONSHU

KYUSHU

SHIKOKU

SAKHALIN

KURIL IS.

RYUKYU ISLANDS

TAIWAN

HAINAN

PALAWAN

MINDANAO

LUZON

HALMAHERA

TIMOR

NICOBAR IS. (INDIA)

ANDAMAN IS. (INDIA)

LACCADIVE IS. (INDIA)

MALDIVE IS.

SOCOTRA I.

CAPE COMORIN

C. NEGRAIS

FRANZ JOSEF LAND

NEW SIBERIAN IS.

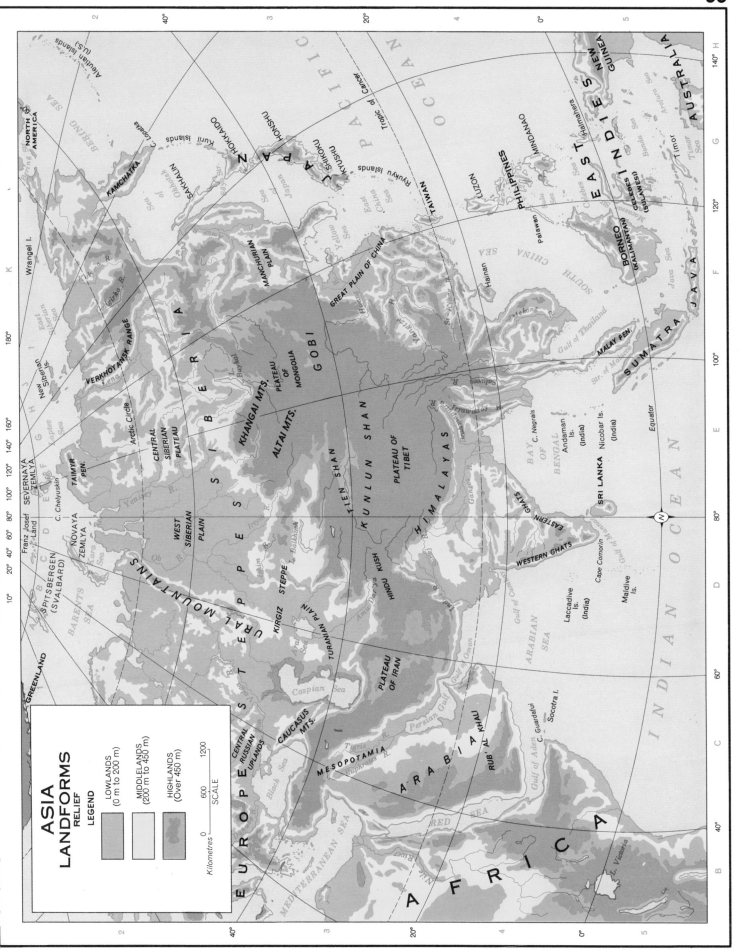

ASIA
LANDFORMS
RELIEF

LEGEND

LOWLANDS
(0 m to 200 m)

MIDDLELANDS
(200 m to 450 m)

HIGHLANDS
(Over 450 m)

SCALE

Kilometres

0   600   1200

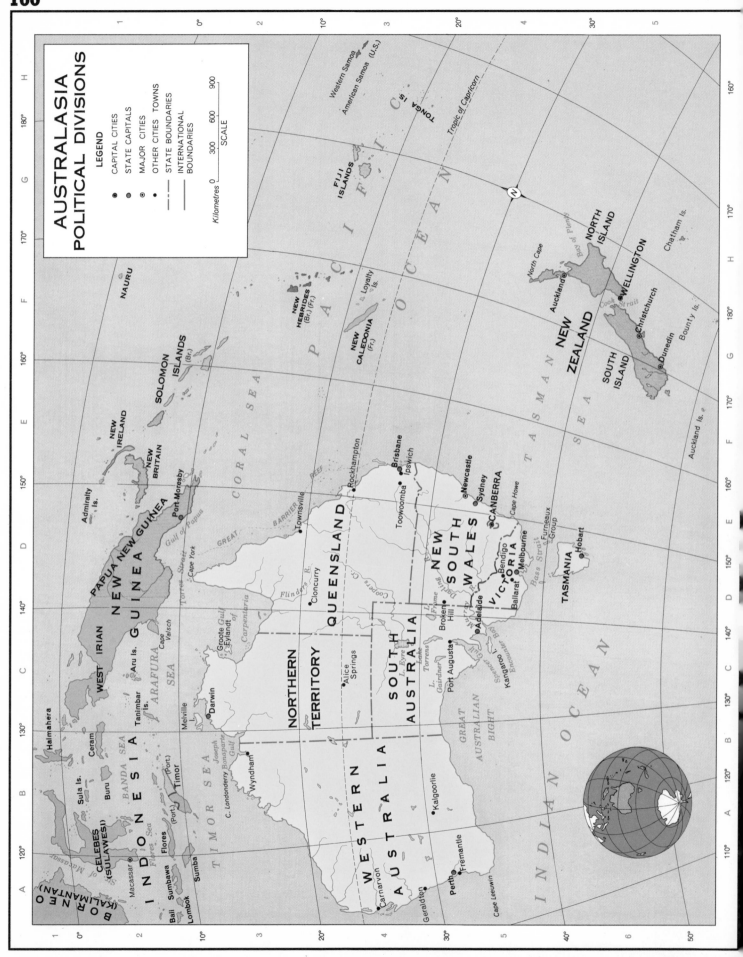

AUSTRALASIA POLITICAL DIVISIONS

LEGEND

- ● CAPITAL CITIES
- ◉ STATE CAPITALS
- ◎ MAJOR CITIES
- • OTHER CITIES TOWNS
- —·—· STATE BOUNDARIES
- ——— INTERNATIONAL BOUNDARIES

Kilometres 0 300 600 900
SCALE

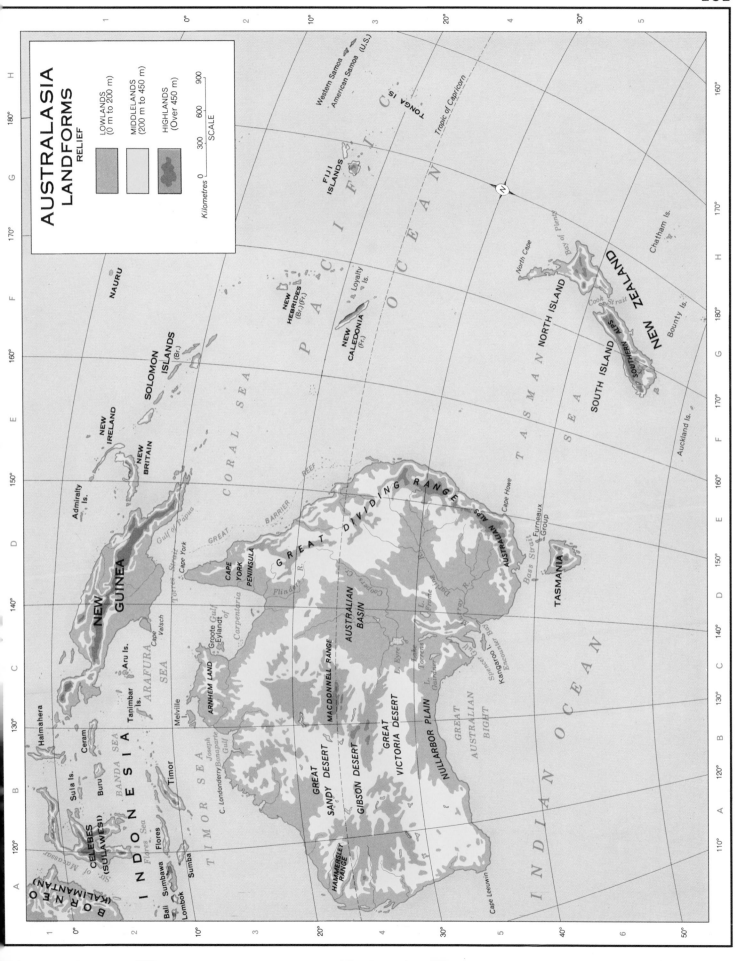

AUSTRALASIA
LANDFORMS
RELIEF

LOWLANDS
(0 m to 200 m)

MIDDLELANDS
(200 m to 450 m)

HIGHLANDS
(Over 450 m)

SCALE

Kilometres 0 300 600 900

BORNEO
(KALIMANTAN)

CELEBES
(SULAWESI)

I N D O N E S I A

Halmahera

Sula Is.

Ceram

Buru

BANDA SEA

Flores Sea

Flores

Bali

Sumbawa

Lombok

Sumba

Timor

Melville I.

C. Londonderry

TIMOR SEA

Tanimbar Is.

Aru Is.

Cape Valsch

ARAFURA SEA

NEW GUINEA

Admiralty Is.

NEW IRELAND

NEW BRITAIN

SOLOMON ISLANDS

NAURU

Gulf of Papua

Torres Strait

Cape York

GREAT

BARRIER

REEF

CORAL SEA

Joseph Bonaparte Gulf

ARNHEM LAND

Groote Eylandt

Gulf of Carpentaria

CAPE YORK PENINSULA

Flinders R.

GREAT SANDY DESERT

GIBSON DESERT

GREAT VICTORIA DESERT

NULLARBOR PLAIN

HAMMERSLEY RANGE

MACDONNELL RANGE

AUSTRALIAN BASIN

Cooper's Cr.

L. Eyre

L. Torrens

L. Gairdner

Spencer Bay

Kangaroo I.

Encounter Bay

GREAT AUSTRALIAN BIGHT

GREAT DIVIDING RANGE

Darling R.

Murray R.

L. Frome

Murrumbidgee R.

Cape Howe

AUSTRALIAN ALPS

Furneaux Group

Bass Strait

TASMANIA

Cape Leeuwin

I N D I A N   O C E A N

P A C I F I C   O C E A N

Western Samoa

American Samoa (U.S.)

TONGA IS.

Tropic of Capricorn

FIJI ISLANDS

NEW HEBRIDES (Br.)(Fr.)

NEW CALEDONIA (Fr.)

Loyalty Is.

T A S M A N   S E A

North Cape

Bay of Plenty

NORTH ISLAND

Cook Strait

SOUTHERN ALPS

SOUTH ISLAND

NEW ZEALAND

Chatham Is.

Bounty Is.

Auckland Is.

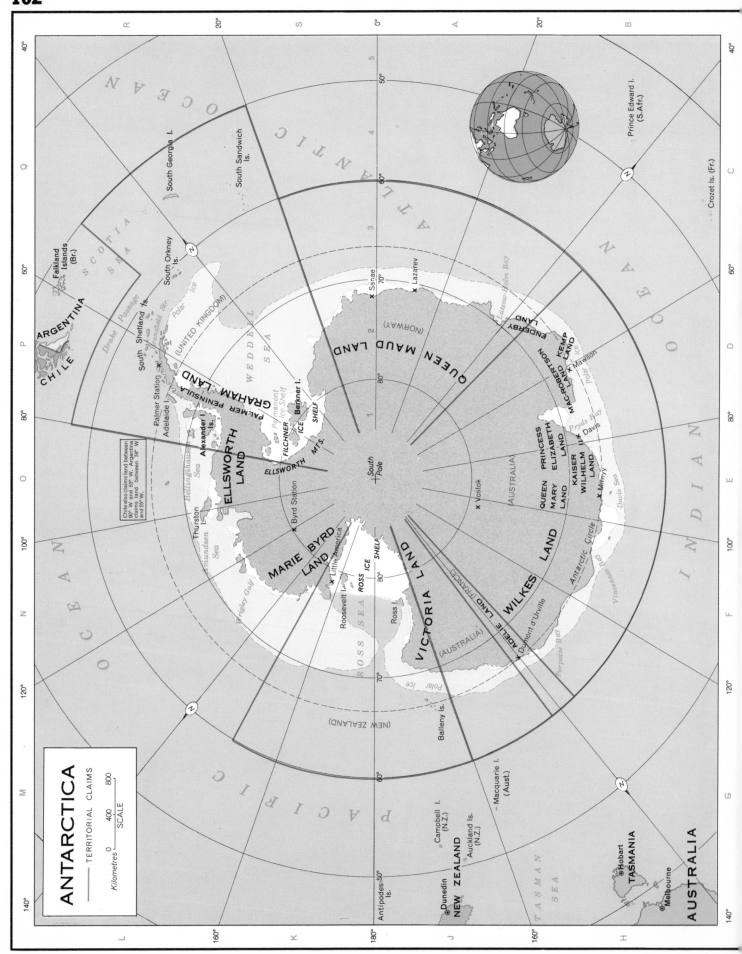

ANTARCTICA

TERRITORIAL CLAIMS

Kilometres
0   400   800
SCALE

Falkland Islands (Br.)

South Georgia I.

South Sandwich Is.

ARGENTINA

CHILE

SCOTIA SEA

Drake Passage

South Orkney Is.

South Shetland Is.

Palmer Station ×
Adelaide I.

Alexander I.

Bransfield Str.

Polar Ice

WEDDELL SEA

(UNITED KINGDOM)

GRAHAM LAND

PALMER PENINSULA

Permanent Ice Shelf

Filchner Ice Shelf

Berkner I.

ELLSWORTH MTS.

FILCHNER ICE SHELF

Chile also claims land between 90° W and 53° W. Argentina claims land between 74° W and 25° W.

Bellingshausen Sea

ELLSWORTH LAND

Thurston I.

Amundsen Sea

Byrd Station ×

MARIE BYRD LAND

Little America ×

Roosevelt I.

Ross I.

ROSS SEA

ROSS ICE SHELF

Virgley Gulf

South Pole

× Vostok

(AUSTRALIA)

QUEEN MAUD LAND
(NORWAY)

× Sanae

× Lazarev

Lützow-Holm Bay

ENDERBY LAND

KEMP LAND

MAC-ROBERTSON LAND

× Mawson

Polar Ice

Prydz Bay

QUEEN MARY LAND

PRINCESS ELIZABETH LAND

KAISER WILHELM II LAND

× Mirny
× Davis

Davis Sea

WILKES LAND

Antarctic Circle

Vincennes Bay

Porpoise Bay

× Dumont d'Urville

ADÉLIE LAND (FRANCE)

VICTORIA LAND

(AUSTRALIA)

(NEW ZEALAND)

Balleny Is.

Macquarie I. (Aust.)

Prince Edward I. (S.Afr.)

Crozet Is. (Fr.)

ATLANTIC OCEAN

INDIAN OCEAN

PACIFIC OCEAN

TASMAN SEA

Campbell I. (N.Z.)

Auckland Is. (N.Z.)

Antipodes Is.

Dunedin ⊙ NEW ZEALAND

Hobart ⊙ TASMANIA

Melbourne ⊙

AUSTRALIA

20° 0° 20° 40° 60° 80° 100° 120° 140° 160° 180°

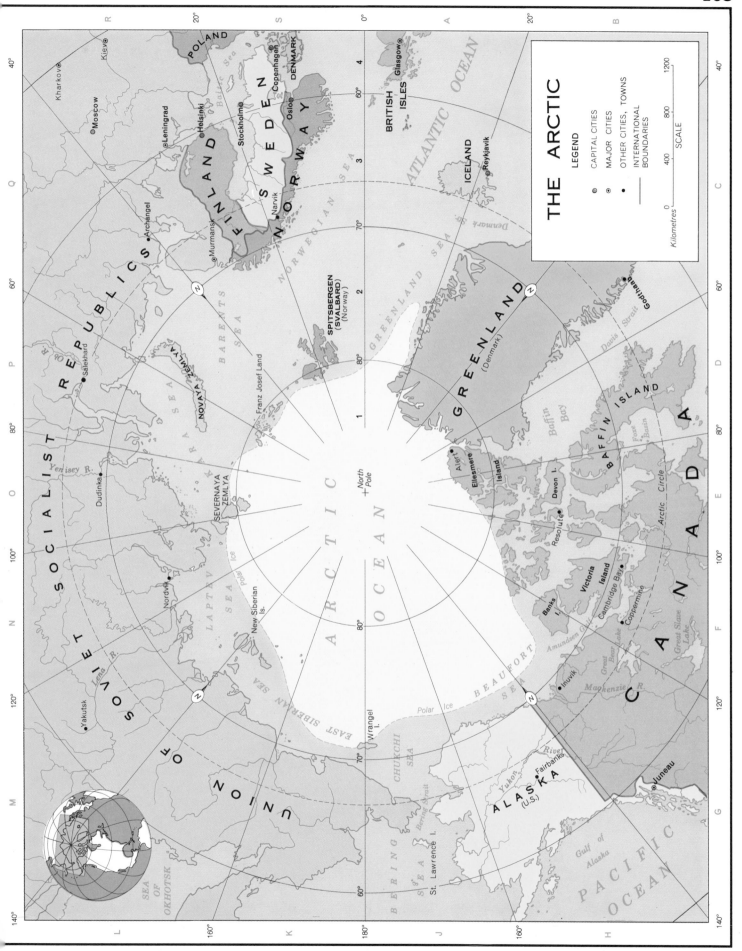

THE ARCTIC

LEGEND

CAPITAL CITIES

MAJOR CITIES

OTHER CITIES, TOWNS

INTERNATIONAL BOUNDARIES

SCALE

Kilometres

0 400 800 1200

ATLANTIC OCEAN

BRITISH ISLES

Glasgow

ICELAND

Reykjavik

Denmark Str.

GREENLAND
(Denmark)

Godthaab

Davis Strait

Baffin Bay

BAFFIN ISLAND

Fox Basin

Alert

Ellesmere Island

Devon I.

Resolute

Arctic Circle

Victoria Island

Cambridge Bay

Coppermine

Banks I.

Great Bear Lake

Amundsen G.

Great Slave Lake

CANADA

Mackenzie R.

Inuvik

Great Bear R.

BEAUFORT SEA

Yukon River

Fairbanks

ALASKA
(U.S.)

Juneau

Gulf of Alaska

PACIFIC OCEAN

BERING SEA

St. Lawrence I.

Bering Strait

CHUKCHI SEA

Wrangel I.

Polar Ice

ARCTIC OCEAN

North Pole

EAST SIBERIAN SEA

Polar Ice

New Siberian Is.

LAPTEV SEA

Nordvik

Lena R.

Yakutsk

UNION OF SOVIET SOCIALIST REPUBLICS

SEA OF OKHOTSK

SEVERNAYA ZEMLYA

Dudinka

Yenisey R.

Salekhard

KARA SEA

NOVAYA ZEMLYA

Franz Josef Land

BARENTS SEA

Murmansk

Archangel

Kharkov

Moscow

Kiev

Leningrad

Helsinki

FINLAND

Stockholm

SWEDEN

Baltic Sea

POLAND

Copenhagen

DENMARK

Oslo

NORWAY

Narvik

NORWEGIAN SEA

SPITSBERGEN
(SVALBARD)
(Norway)

GREENLAND SEA

Arctic Circle

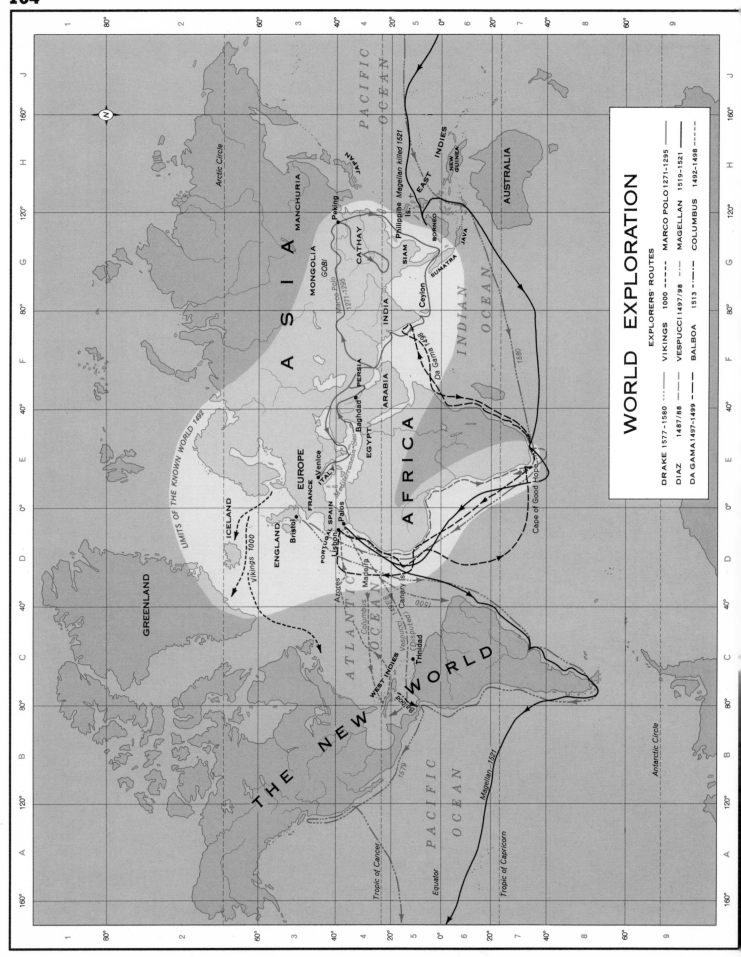

WORLD EXPLORATION

EXPLORERS' ROUTES

DRAKE 1577–1580	VIKINGS 1000	MARCO POLO 1271–1295
DIAZ 1487/88	VESPUCCI 1497/98	MAGELLAN 1519–1521
DA GAMA 1497–1499	BALBOA 1513	COLUMBUS 1492–1498

PACIFIC OCEAN

Arctic Circle

MANCHURIA

A S I A

MONGOLIA

GOBI

Marco Polo 1271–1295

CATHAY

Peking

N₂
JAP₄

Philippine Magellan killed 1521

EAST INDIES

NEW GUINEA

SIAM

Borneo

JAVA

SUMATRA

Ceylon

INDIA

PERSIA

Baghdad

ARABIA

Da Gama 1498

EGYPT

AFRICA

INDIAN OCEAN

1580

AUSTRALIA

Mediterranean Sea

EUROPE

Venice

ITALY

FRANCE

ENGLAND

Bristol

PORTUGAL SPAIN

Lisbon Palos

Azores

Madeira

Canary Is.

Cape of Good Hope

ICELAND

Vikings 1000

GREENLAND

LIMITS OF THE KNOWN WORLD 1492

ATLANTIC OCEAN

Columbus

Vespucci
(Disputed)

1500

Trinidad

WEST INDIES

THE NEW WORLD

PACIFIC OCEAN

1579

Magellan 1521

Tropic of Cancer

Equator

Tropic of Capricorn

Antarctic Circle

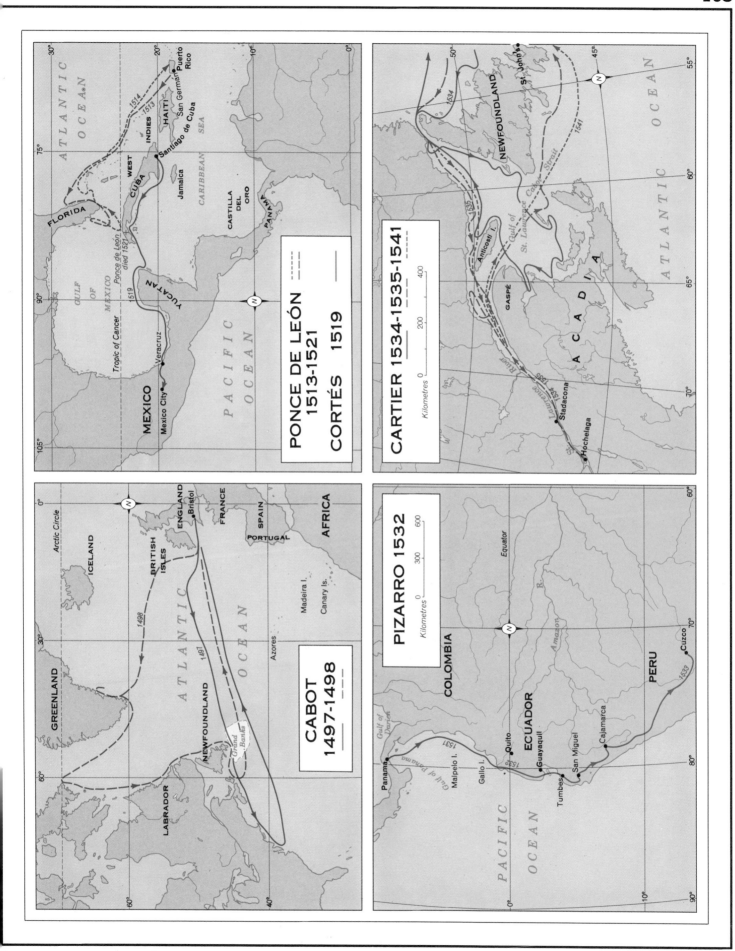

PONCE DE LEÓN 1513-1521

CORTÉS 1519

CARTIER 1534-1535-1541

CABOT 1497-1498

PIZARRO 1532

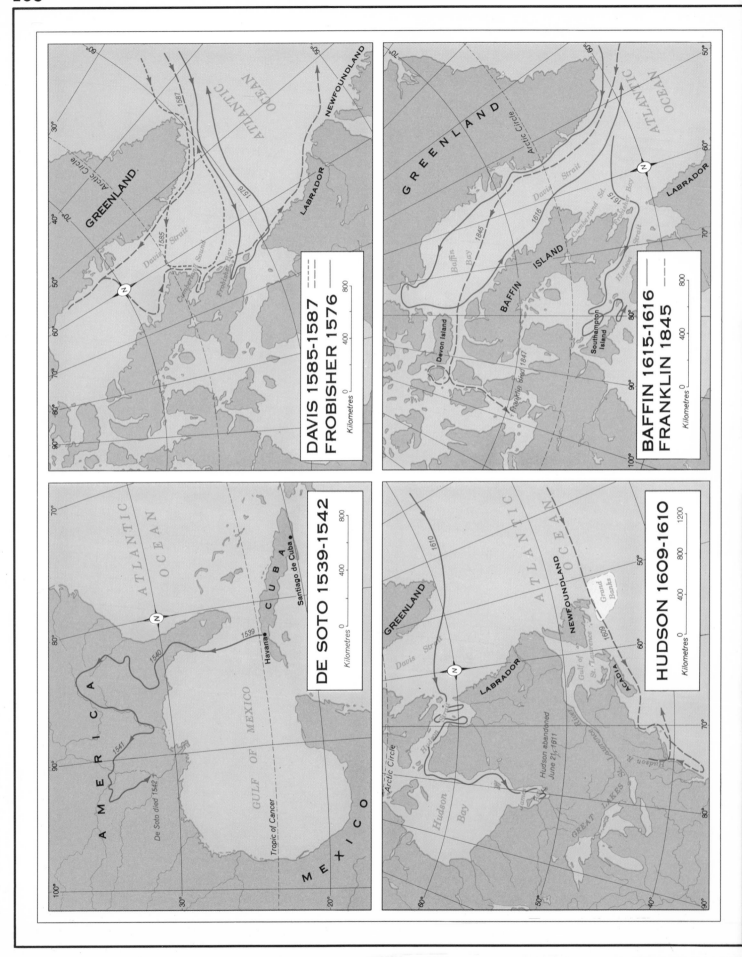

DAVIS 1585-1587
FROBISHER 1576

BAFFIN 1615-1616
FRANKLIN 1845

DE SOTO 1539-1542

HUDSON 1609-1610

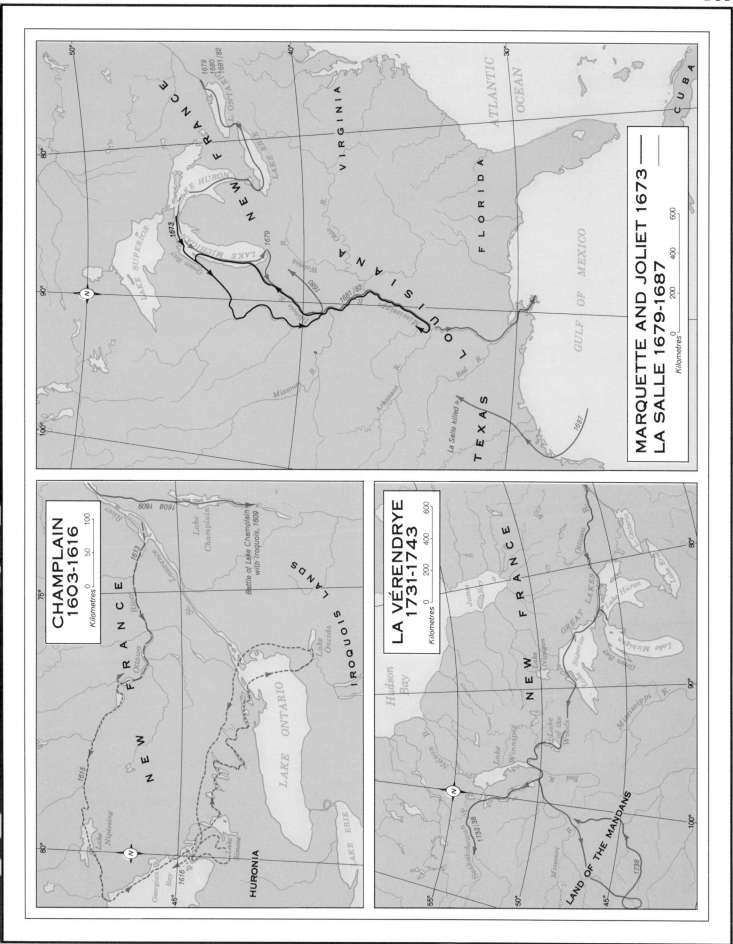

MARQUETTE AND JOLIET 1673
LA SALLE 1679-1687

CHAMPLAIN
1603-1616

LA VÉRENDRYE
1731-1743

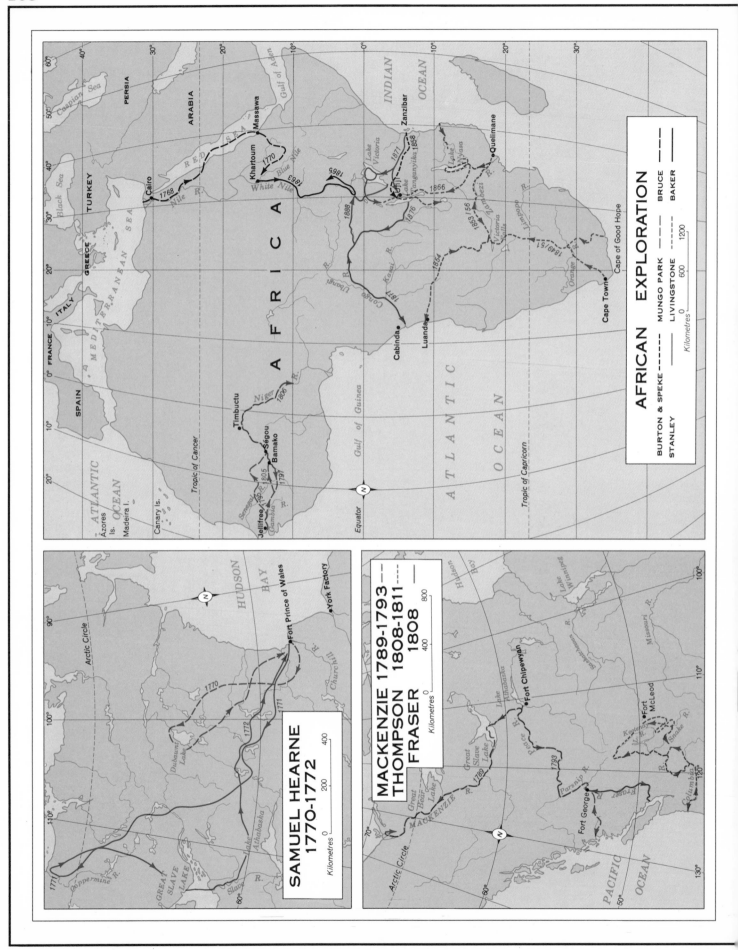

AFRICAN EXPLORATION

BURTON & SPEKE -----   MUNGO PARK -----   BRUCE ----

STANLEY ——   LIVINGSTONE ——   BAKER ----

Kilometres 0   600   1200

SAMUEL HEARNE 1770-1772

Kilometres 0   200   400

MACKENZIE 1789-1793
THOMPSON 1808-1811
FRASER 1808

Kilometres 0   400   800

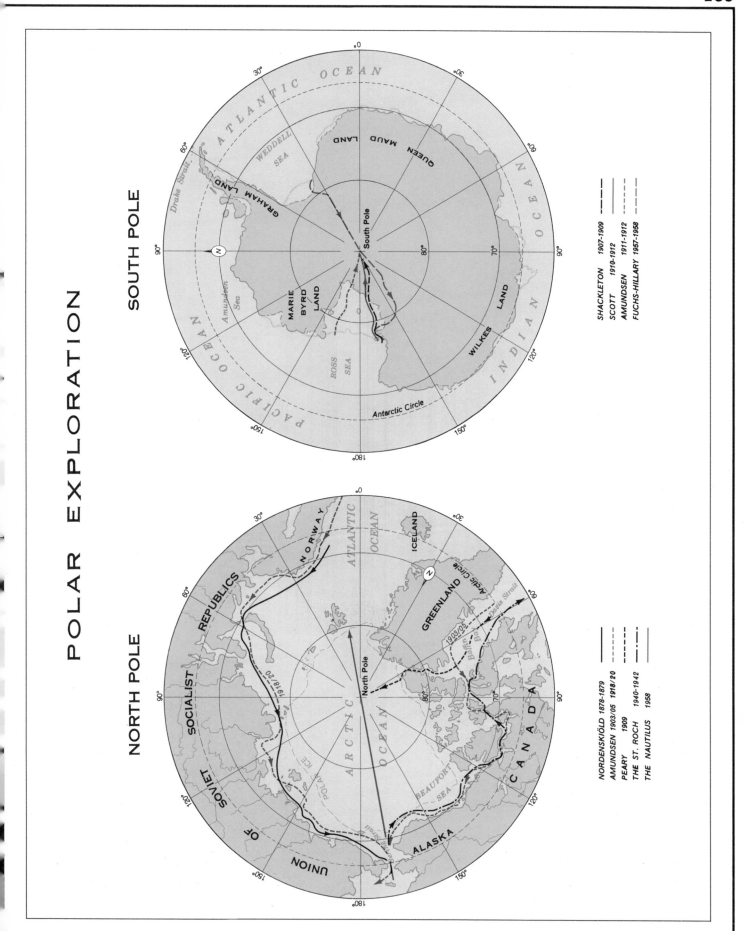

POLAR EXPLORATION

SOUTH POLE

NORTH POLE

SHACKLETON 1907-1909
SCOTT 1910-1912
AMUNDSEN 1911-1912
FUCHS-HILLARY 1957-1958

NORDENSKIÖLD 1878-1879
AMUNDSEN 1903/05 1918/20
PEARY 1909
THE ST. ROCH 1940-1942
THE NAUTILUS 1958

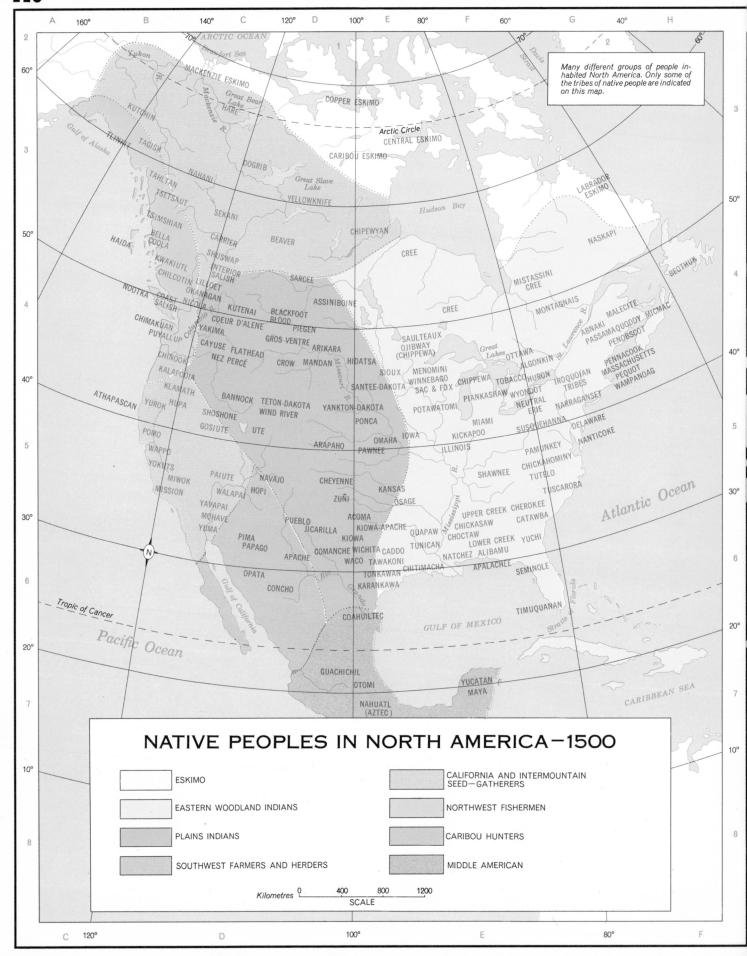

A | 160° | B | 140° | C | 120° | D | 100° | E | 80° | F | 60° | G | 40° | H

Many different groups of people inhabited North America. Only some of the tribes of native people are indicated on this map.

ARCTIC OCEAN
Beaufort Sea
Yukon R.
MACKENZIE ESKIMO
KUTCHIN
Great Bear Lake
HARE
COPPER ESKIMO
Arctic Circle
CENTRAL ESKIMO
CARIBOU ESKIMO
Mackenzie R.
TLINGIT
TAGISH
TAHLTAN
NAHANI
TSETSAUT
DOGRIB
TSIMSHIAN
SEKANI
YELLOWKNIFE
Great Slave Lake
Hudson Bay
LABRADOR ESKIMO
HAIDA
BELLA COOLA
CARRIER
BEAVER
CHIPEWYAN
NASKAPI
KWAKIUTL
SHUSWAP
CREE
MISTASSINI CREE
BEOTHUK
CHILCOTIN LILLOET
INTERIOR SALISH
SARCEE
CREE
MONTAGNAIS
NOOTKA
OKANAGAN
COAST NICOLA SALISH
KUTENAI
ASSINIBOINE
St. Lawrence R.
ABNAKI MALECITE
CHIMAKUAN
YAKIMA
BLACKFOOT
BLOOD
PIEGEN
GROS-VENTRE
ARIKARA
SAULTEAUX OJIBWAY (CHIPPEWA)
Great Lakes
OTTAWA
ALGONKIN
PASSAMAQUODDY MICMAC
PENOBSCOT
PUYALLUP
COEUR D'ALENE
CAYUSE FLATHEAD
NEZ PERCÉ
CROW MANDAN
HIDATSA
MENOMINI
WINNEBAGO
SAC & FOX
CHIPPEWA
TOBACCO
HURON
IROQUOIAN TRIBES
PENNACOOK
MASSACHUSETTS
PEQUOT
WAMPANOAG
CHINOOK
KALAPODIA
BANNOCK
TETON-DAKOTA
WIND RIVER
SIOUX
SANTEE-DAKOTA
YANKTON-DAKOTA
PIANKASHAW
WYONDOT
NEUTRAL
ERIE
NARRAGANSET
KLAMATH
ATHAPASCAN
YUROK
HUPA
SHOSHONE
GOSIUTE
UTE
PONCA
OMAHA
IOWA
POTAWATOMI
MIAMI
KICKAPOO
SUSQUEHANNA
DELAWARE
NANTICOKE
POMO
WAPPO
ARAPAHO
PAWNEE
ILLINOIS
PAMUNKEY
CHICKAHOMINY
TUTELO
YOKUTS
MIWOK
PAIUTE
NAVAJO
CHEYENNE
KANSAS
SHAWNEE
TUSCARORA
MISSION
WALAPAI
HOPI
ZUÑI
OSAGE
UPPER CREEK CHEROKEE
CATAWBA
YAVAPAI
MOHAVE
YUMA
PUEBLO
JICARILLA
KIOWA
ACOMA
KIOWA-APACHE
QUAPAW
CHICKASAW
CHOCTAW
LOWER CREEK
YUCHI
PIMA PAPAGO
APACHE
COMANCHE WICHITA
WACO TAWAKONI
CADDO
TUNICAN
NATCHEZ ALIBAMU
OPATA
TONKAWAN
CHITIMACHA
APALACHEE
SEMINOLE
CONCHO
KARANKAWA
Rio Grande
GULF OF MEXICO
Straits of Florida
TIMUQUANAN
COAHUILTEC
Gulf of California
Tropic of Cancer
Pacific Ocean
Atlantic Ocean
CARIBBEAN SEA
GUACHICHIL
OTOMI
YUCATAN
MAYA
NAHUATL (AZTEC)

NATIVE PEOPLES IN NORTH AMERICA—1500

ESKIMO

EASTERN WOODLAND INDIANS

PLAINS INDIANS

SOUTHWEST FARMERS AND HERDERS

CALIFORNIA AND INTERMOUNTAIN SEED—GATHERERS

NORTHWEST FISHERMEN

CARIBOU HUNTERS

MIDDLE AMERICAN

Kilometres 0 400 800 1200
SCALE

C | 120° | D | 100° | E | 80° | F

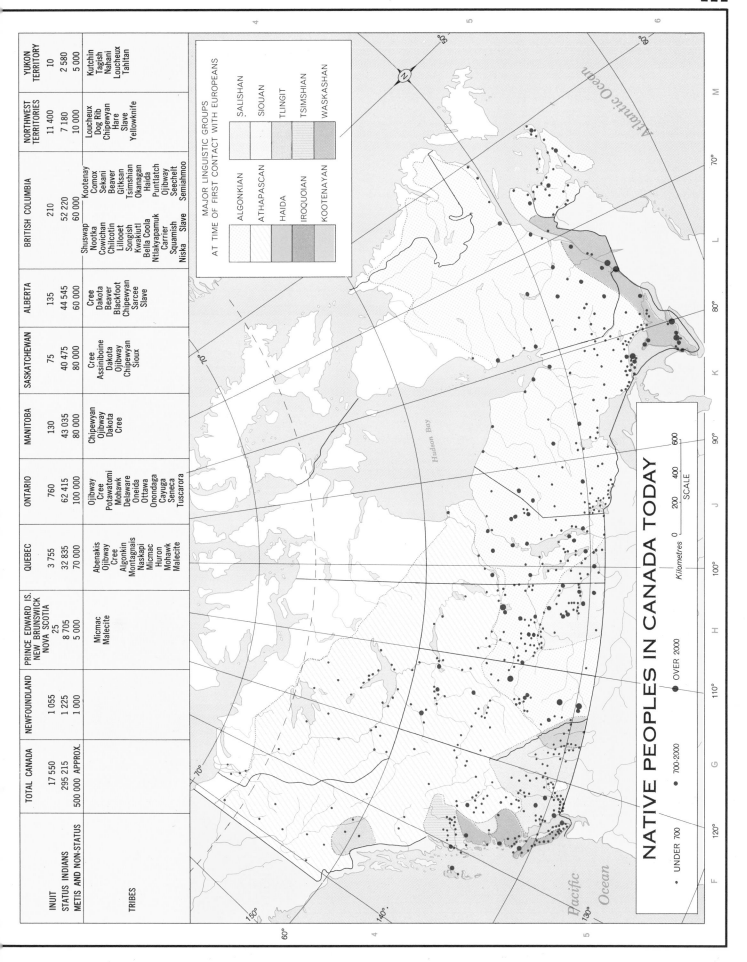

NATIVE PEOPLES IN CANADA TODAY

	TOTAL CANADA	NEWFOUNDLAND	PRINCE EDWARD IS. NEW BRUNSWICK NOVA SCOTIA	QUEBEC	ONTARIO	MANITOBA	SASKATCHEWAN	ALBERTA	BRITISH COLUMBIA	NORTHWEST TERRITORIES	YUKON TERRITORY
INUIT	17 550	1 055		3 755	760	130	75	135	210	11 400	10
STATUS INDIANS	295 215	1 225	8 705	32 835	62 415	43 035	40 475	44 545	52 220	7 180	2 580
METIS AND NON-STATUS	500 000 APPROX.	1 000	5 000	70 000	100 000	80 000	80 000	60 000	60 000	10 000	5 000
TRIBES			Micmac Malecite	Abenakis Ojibway Cree Algonkin Montagnais Naskapi Micmac Huron Mohawk Malecite	Ojibway Cree Potawatomi Mohawk Delaware Oneida Ottawa Onondaga Cayuga Seneca Tuscarora	Chipewyan Ojibway Dakota Cree	Cree Assiniboine Dakota Ojibway Chipewyan Sioux	Cree Dakota Beaver Blackfoot Chipewyan Sarcee Slave	Shuswap Nootka Cowichan Chilcotin Lillooet Songish Kwakiutl Bella Coola Ntlakyapamuk Carrier Squamish Niska Slave Kootenay Comox Sekani Beaver Gitksan Tsimshian Okanagan Haida Puntlatch Ojibway Seechelt Semiahmoo	Loucheux Dog Rib Chipewyan Hare Slave Yellowknife	Kutchin Tagish Nahani Loucheux Tahltan

MAJOR LINGUISTIC GROUPS
AT TIME OF FIRST CONTACT WITH EUROPEANS

ALGONKIAN	SALISHAN
ATHAPASCAN	SIOUAN
HAIDA	TLINGIT
IROQUOIAN	TSIMSHIAN
KOOTENAYAN	WASKASHAN

SCALE

Kilometres 0 200 400 600

• UNDER 700
● 700-2000
⬤ OVER 2000

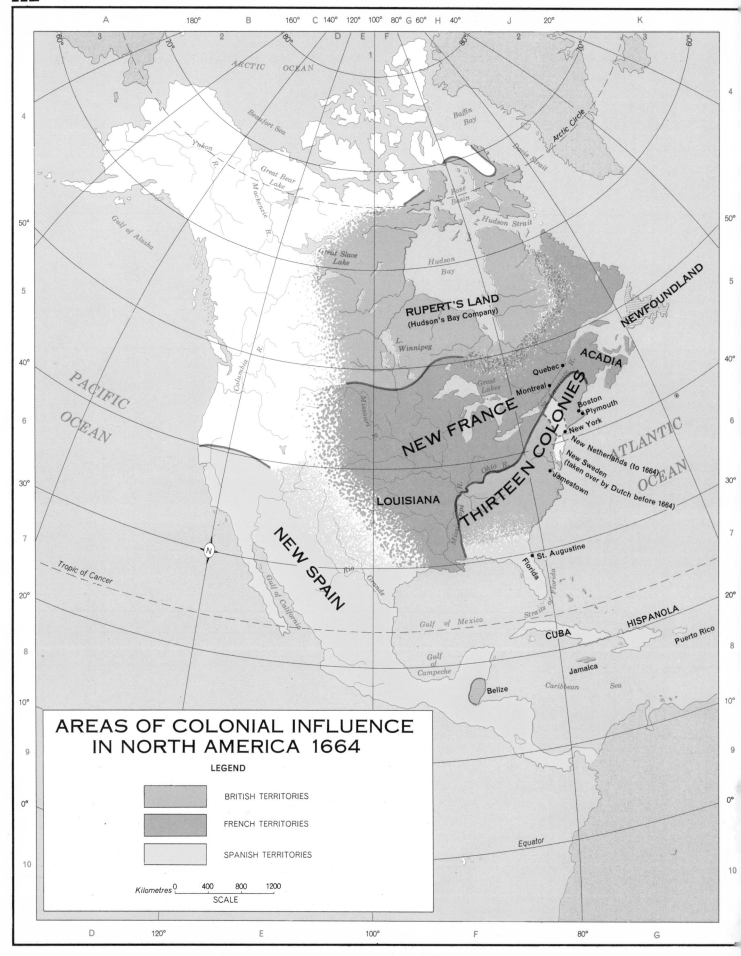

AREAS OF COLONIAL INFLUENCE IN NORTH AMERICA 1664

LEGEND

	BRITISH TERRITORIES
	FRENCH TERRITORIES
	SPANISH TERRITORIES

Kilometres 0 400 800 1200
SCALE

ARCTIC OCEAN

Beaufort Sea

Yukon R.

Great Bear Lake

Mackenzie R.

Baffin Bay

Davis Strait

Arctic Circle

Foxe Basin

Hudson Strait

Great Slave Lake

Hudson Bay

Gulf of Alaska

Columbia R.

RUPERT'S LAND
(Hudson's Bay Company)

L. Winnipeg

NEWFOUNDLAND

PACIFIC OCEAN

Missouri R.

Great Lakes

Quebec

ACADIA

Montreal

NEW FRANCE

Boston
Plymouth
New York
New Netherlands (to 1664)
New Sweden
(taken over by Dutch before 1664)
Jamestown

THIRTEEN COLONIES

ATLANTIC OCEAN

Ohio R.

LOUISIANA

NEW SPAIN

Rio Grande

Gulf of California

St. Augustine

Florida

Straits of Florida

Tropic of Cancer

Gulf of Mexico

CUBA

HISPANOLA

Puerto Rico

Gulf of Campeche

Jamaica

Belize

Caribbean Sea

Equator

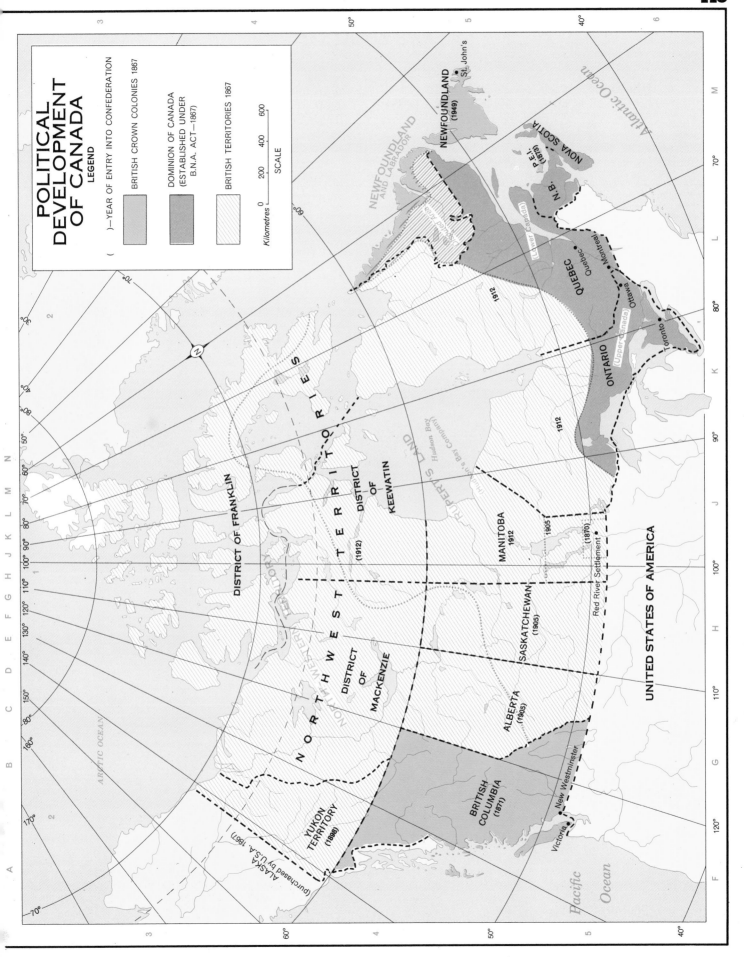

POLITICAL
DEVELOPMENT
OF CANADA

LEGEND

( )—YEAR OF ENTRY INTO CONFEDERATION

BRITISH CROWN COLONIES 1867

DOMINION OF CANADA
(ESTABLISHED UNDER
B.N.A. ACT—1867)

BRITISH TERRITORIES 1867

SCALE

Kilometres

0   200   400   600

Atlantic Ocean

St. John's

NEWFOUNDLAND
(1949)

NEWFOUNDLAND
AND LABRADOR

NOVA SCOTIA

P.E.I.
(1873)

N.B.

(Lower Canada)

QUEBEC

Quebec
Montreal

Ottawa

1912

ONTARIO

(Upper Canada)

Toronto

1912

NORTH WEST TERRITORIES

DISTRICT OF FRANKLIN

DISTRICT
OF
KEEWATIN

(1912)

Hudson Bay

RUPERT'S LAND

(Hudson's Bay Company)

MANITOBA
1912

1905

(1870)

DISTRICT
OF
MACKENZIE

SASKATCHEWAN
(1905)

Red River Settlement

UNITED STATES OF AMERICA

ALBERTA
(1905)

BRITISH
COLUMBIA
(1871)

New Westminster

Victoria

YUKON
TERRITORY
(1898)

ALASKA
(purchased by U.S.A. 1867)

ARCTIC OCEAN

Pacific
Ocean

Gazetteer

On the following pages are two alphabetical lists of all the important names that appear on the maps in this atlas. The first list is of Canadian names, and the other is of the rest of the world.

Names are generally followed by the name of the country, continent, or ocean in which they are situated. The Canadian names, however, are not followed by the name of the country, but they do include the name of the province in which the place is found. Those names that appear more than once are indexed only once, to the map on which they are most easily located.

After each name there is a figure that shows the page number of the map on which you will find the place. Following this is a letter and another figure. These refer to the letters along the top and bottom of each map and to the figures along each side. Together they will help you find the position of any place on the map.

Physical features as well as places are listed in the gazetteer. Each feature named is followed by a term indicating its nature, and abbreviated as shown on page 115.

Names appearing more than once are listed in this order: first, place names; second, political divisions; and third, physical features.

Abbreviations

Afghan.	Afghanistan	Guat.	Guatemala	Pac. Oc.	Pacific Ocean
Ala.	Alabama	Hon.	Honduras	Pak.	Pakistan
Alsk.	Alaska			P.E.I.	Prince Edward Island
Alta.	Alberta	i., is., Is.	island(s)	pen.	peninsula
Antarc.	Antarctica	Ill.	Illinois	Port.	Portuguese
arch.	archipelago	in.	inlet	prov.	province
Arc. Oc.	Arctic Ocean	Ind. Oc.	Indian Ocean	pt.	point
Ariz.	Arizona	isth.	isthmus		
At. Oc.	Atlantic Ocean			Que.	Quebec
Aust.	Australia	l., L., ls.	lake(s)		
		Louis.	Louisiana	r.	river
b.	bay			reg.	region
bas.	basin	Man.	Manitoba	rep., Rep.	republic
B.C.	British Columbia	Mass.	Massachusetts	res.	reservoir
		Md.	Maryland	res. stat.	research station
c.	cape	Med. S.	Mediterranean Sea	Rhod.	Rhodesia
Calif.	California	Mex.	Mexico		
C. Am.	Central America	Mich.	Michigan	s.	sea
Can.	Canada	Minn.	Minnesota	S.	South
Carib. S.	Caribbean Sea	Miss.	Mississippi	S. Am.	South America
ch., Ch.	channel	Mon. Rep.	Mongolian Republic	Sask.	Saskatchewan
Congo		mt., Mt.,		S.C.	South Carolina
Rep.	Congo Republic	mts.	mountain(s)	sd.	sound
Conn.	Connecticut			S.D.	South Dakota
cur.	current	N.	North, Northern; New	Sp.	Spain, Spanish
Czech.	Czechoslovakia	N. Am.	North America	St., Ste.	Saint
		N.B.	New Brunswick	str.	strait
Dem.	Democratic	N.C.	North Carolina	S.W.	South West
Den.	Denmark	N.D.	North Dakota	Switz.	Switzerland
des.	desert	Neb.	Nebraska		
dist.	district	Neth.	Netherlands	Tas.	Tasmania
Dom. Rep.	Dominican	Nfld.	Newfoundland	Tenn.	Tennessee
	Republic	N.H.	New Hampshire	terr. Terr.	territory
D.R. Congo	Democratic	Nic.	Nicaragua	Tex.	Texas
	Republic of	N.J.	New Jersey		
	the Congo	N. Mex.	New Mexico	U.S.A.	United States of
		N.S.	Nova Scotia		America
Eur.	Europe	N.W.T.	Northwest Territories	U.S.S.R.	Union of Soviet
		N.Y.	New York		Socialist Republics
f.	feature	N.Z.	New Zealand		
Fla.	Florida			Venez.	Venezuela
Fr.	France, French	Okla.	Oklahoma		
		Ont.	Ontario	W.	West
g.	gulf			Wash.	Washington
G. of Mex.	Gulf of Mexico	Pa.	Pennsylvania	W. Virg.	West Virginia

Canada

North, *c.*, N.S.	51	E2
North Battleford, Sask.	71	E4
North Bay, Ont.	64	E3
Northern Indian, *l.*, Man.	67	D2
North Knife, *r.*, Man.	67	E1
North Mountain, N.S.	52	C3
North Point, *c.*, P.E.I.	51	C2
N. Saskatchewan, *r.*, Alta./Sask.	44	H4
Northumberland, *str.*	51	D2
North Vancouver, B.C.	79	D3
Northwest Territories, *terr.*	40	J3
Norway House, Man.	67	D4
Notre Dame, *b.*, Nfld.	48	D3
Notre Dame, *mts.*, Que.	57	D4
Nottawasaga, *b.*, Ont.	60	B2
Nottawasaga, *r.*, Ont.	60	C2
Nottaway, *r.*, Que.	56	B3
Nova Scotia, *prov.*	40	M5
Nueltin, *l.*, Man./N.W.T.	83	E3
Oakville, Ont.	60	C3
Ocean Falls, B.C.	82	C2
Oil Springs	63	A3
Okanagan, *l.*, B.C.	79	E2
Okanagan, *r.*, B.C.	79	E3
Old Crow, Yukon	83	C3
Oldman, *r.*, Alta.	75	F6
Old Wives, *l.*, Sask.	67	D3
Omineca, *mts.*, B.C.	80	C1
Ontario, *prov.*	40	K4
Ontario, *l.*	44	L5
Orillia, Ont.	60	C2
Oshawa, Ont.	60	C3
Otish, *mts.*, Que.	57	C3
Ottawa, Ont.	60	E2
Ottawa, *is.*, N.W.T.	83	E4
Ottawa, *r.*, Ont./Que.	44	L5
Outardes, R. aux, *r.*, Que.	59	D2
Outlook, Sask.	71	F5
Owen Sound, Ont.	60	B2
Oxford, *l.*, Man.	67	E3
Oxford House, Man.	67	E3
Pacific Ocean	34	D6
Pangnirtung, N.W.T.	83	F3
Parrsboro, N.S.	51	C3
Parry Sound, Ont.	60	B2
Parsnip, *r.*, B.C.	79	D1
Pas, The, Man.	67	B4
Passamaquoddy, *b.*, N.B.	51	B3
Paulatuk, N.W.T.	83	C3
Payne, *r.*, Que.	56	C1
Payne Bay, Que.	56	D1
Peace, *r.*, Alta.	75	D2
Peace River, Alta.	75	D2
Peel, *r.*, Yukon	83	C3
Pelee, *i.*, Ont.	60	A4
Pelee, *pt.*, Ont.	60	A4
Pelican, *mts.*, Alta.	76	E3
Pelly, *r.*, Yukon	83	C3
Pelly Bay, N.W.T.	83	E3
Pembina, *r.*, Alta.	75	E4
Pembina, *r.*, Man./U.S.A.	67	C6
Pembroke, Ont.	60	D2
Penticton, B.C.	79	E3
Peribonca, *r.*, Que.	56	C4
Perth, N.B.	51	B2
Perth, Ont.	60	D2
Petawawa, *r.*, Ont.	60	D1
Peterborough, Ont.	60	C2

Peter Pond, *l.*, Sask.	71	E2
Petit Nord, *pen.*, Nfld.	49	C2
Petrolia, Ont.	63	A3
Pickle Crow, Ont.	64	C2
Picton, Ont.	60	D2
Pictou, N.S.	51	D3
Pincher Creek, Alta.	75	F6
Pine Falls, Man.	67	D5
Pinehouse, *l.*, Sask.	71	F3
Pine Point, N.W.T.	83	D3
Pipestone, *r.*, Ont.	64	B2
Placentia, Nfld.	48	E4
Placentia, *b.*, Nfld.	48	D4
Playgreen, *l.*, Man.	67	C3
Pond Inlet, N.W.T.	83	F2
Ponoka, Alta.	75	F4
Poplar, *r.*, Man.	67	D4
Porcupine, *r.*, Yukon/Alsk.	83	B3
Portage la Prairie, Man.	67	C6
Port Alberni, B.C.	79	D3
Port-aux-Basques, Nfld.	48	B4
Port Cartier, Que.	56	D3
Port Colborne, Ont.	60	C3
Port Credit, Ont.	63	C3
Port Dalhousie, Ont.	84	Map 1
Port Harrison, Que.	56	B2
Port Hawkesbury, N.S.	51	E3
Port Hope, Ont.	60	C3
Port Radium, N.W.T.	83	D3
Port Robinson, Ont.	84	Map 1
Port Saunders, Nfld.	48	C2
Port Weller, Ont.	84	Map 1
Povungnituk, Que.	83	F3
Powell River, B.C.	82	D3
Prescott, Ont.	84	Map 2
Primrose, *l.*, Sask.	71	E3
Prince Albert, Sask.	71	G4
Prince Charles, *i.*, N.W.T.	83	F3
Prince Edward Island, *prov.*	40	M5
Prince George, B.C.	79	D2
Prince Gustav Adolf, *s.*, N.W.T.	83	D2
Prince of Wales, *i.*, N.W.T.	83	E2
Prince Patrick, *i.*, N.W.T.	40	G2
Prince Regent, *in.*, N.W.T.	83	E2
Prince Rupert, B.C.	79	B2
Princess Royal, *i.*, B.C.	79	C2
Pugwash, N.S.	51	D3
Purcell, *mts.*, B.C.	80	E3
Qu'Appelle, *r.*, Sask.	71	H5
Quebec, *prov.*	40	L4
Queen Charlotte, *is.*, B.C.	79	B2
Queen Charlotte, *sd.*, B.C.	79	C2
Queen Charlotte, *str.*, B.C.	79	C2
Queen Elizabeth, *is.*, N.W.T.	40	H3
Queen Maud, *g.*, N.W.T.	83	D3
Quesnel, B.C.	79	D2
Quesnel, *l.*, B.C.	79	D2
Quill, *ls.*, Sask.	71	G5
Race, *c.*, Nfld.	48	E4
Rae, N.W.T.	83	D3
Rae Lakes, N.W.T.	83	D3
Rainy, *l.*, Ont.	64	B3
Rainy, *r.*, Can./U.S.A.	64	B3
Rainy River, Ont.	64	B3
Raisin, *r.*, Ont.	84	Map 2
Rankin Inlet, N.W.T.	83	E3
Ray, *c.*, Nfld.	48	B4

Read Island, N.W.T.	83	D3
Red, *l.*, Ont.	64	B2
Red, *r.*, Can./U.S.A.	44	J5
Red Deer, Alta.	75	F4
Red Deer, *r.*, Alta.	75	F5
Red Deer, *r.*, Sask./Man.	71	H4
Red Indian, *l.*, Nfld.	48	C3
Red Lake, Ont.	64	B2
Regina, Sask.	71	G5
Reindeer, *i.*, Man.	67	C4
Reindeer, *l.*, Sask./Man.	71	H2
Reliance, N.W.T.	83	D3
Renfrew, Ont.	60	D2
Repulse Bay, N.W.T.	83	E3
Resolute, N.W.T.	83	E2
Resolution, *i.*, N.W.T.	56	E1
Restigouche, *r.*, N.B.	51	B2
Revelstoke, B.C.	79	E2
Rice, *l.*, Ont.	60	C2
Richelieu, *r.*, Que.	56	C4
Rideau, *ls.*, Ont.	60	D2
Rideau, *r.*, Ont.	60	E2
Rimouski, Que.	56	D4
River Jordan, B.C.	79	D3
Rivière du Loup, Que.	56	D4
Roberval, Que.	56	C4
Roblin, Man.	67	B5
Rocher River, N.W.T.	83	D3
Rocky, *mts.*, Can./U.S.A.	35	E5
Rocky Mountain House, Alta.	75	E4
Rocky Mt. Trench, *f.*, B.C.	80	E2
Rodney, Ont.	63	B3
Roes Welcome, *sd.*, N.W.T.	83	E3
Romaine, *r.*, Que.	56	E3
Rosetown, Sask.	71	E5
Rouyn, Que.	56	B4
Rupert, *r.*, Que.	56	B3
Rupert House, Que.	56	B3
Sable, *c.*, N.S.	51	C4
Sable, *i.*, At. Oc.	54	D3
Sachs Harbour, N.W.T.	83	C2
Sackville, N.B.	51	C3
Saguenay, *r.*, Que.	57	C4
St. Andrews, N.B.	51	B3
St. Anthony, Nfld.	48	D2
St. Augustin, *r.*, Que.	56	F3
St. Boniface, Man.	67	D6
St. Catharines, Ont.	60	C3
St. Clair, *l.*, Can./U.S.A.	44	K5
St. Clair, *r.*, Can./U.S.A.	60	A3
St. Croix, *r.*, Can./U.S.A.	51	B3
St. Francis, *c.*, Nfld.	48	E4
St. Francis, *l.*, Ont./Que.	84	Map 2
St. George, N.B.	51	B3
St. George, *c.*, Nfld.	48	B3
St. George's, Nfld.	48	B3
St. George's, *b.*, Nfld.	56	C4
St. Hyacinthe, Que.	56	C4
St. Ignace, *i.*, Ont.	64	C3
Saint John, N.B.	51	B3
St. John, *b.*, Nfld.	48	C2
St. John, *c.*, Nfld.	48	D3
St. John, *l.*, Que.	56	C4
Saint John, *r.*, N.B.	51	B2
St. John's, Nfld.	48	E4
St. Joseph, *i.*, Ont.	60	A1
St. Joseph, *l.*, Ont.	64	B2
St. Lawrence, Nfld.	50	D4
St. Lawrence, *g.*	44	M5

Budapest, Hungary	96	E4
Buenaventura, Colombia	90	B2
Buenos Aires, Argentina	90	D6
Buffalo, N.Y., U.S.A.	85	F2
Bujumbura, Burundi	94	F6
Bulawayo, Rhodesia	94	F8
Bulgaria, Europe	96	F4
Burma, Asia	98	E3
Buru, i., Indonesia	100	B2
Burundi, Africa	94	G6
Butte, Montana, U.S.A.	85	B2
Byrd Station, res. stat., Antarc.	102	M1
Cabinda, Africa	94	E6
Cadiz, Spain	96	C5
Caicos, i., Bahama Is.	89	D2
Cairo, Egypt	94	G2
Calcutta, India	98	E3
Cali, Colombia	100	B2
California, state, U.S.A.	85	A3
California, cur., Pac. Oc.	37	D6
California, g., Pac. Oc.	87	B2
Callao, Peru	90	B4
Camagüey, Cuba	89	C2
Cambay, g., Ind. Oc.	98	D3
Cambodia, Asia	98	F4
Cameroon, Africa	94	E5
Campbell, i., Pac. Oc.	102	J4
Campeche, Mex.	87	F4
Campeche, g., G. of Mex.	34	F4
Campos, f., S. Am.	91	E3
Canadian, r., U.S.A.	86	C3
Canal Zone, Panama	88	D3
Canary, is., At. Oc.	94	B3
Canaveral, c., Fla., U.S.A.	85	E4
Canberra, Aust.	100	D5
Can Phumo, Mozambique	94	G8
Canton, China	98	F3
Cape Horn, cur.	93	A6
Cape Town, Rep. of S. Africa	94	E9
Cape Verde, is., At. Oc.	26	
Cape York, pen., Aust.	101	D3
Cap-Haïtien, Haiti	89	D3
Caracas, Venezuela	90	C1
Caratasca Lagoon, Hon.	88	C1
Cárdenas, Cuba	89	B2
Caribbean, cur., Carib. S.	37	G8
Caribbean, s., At. Oc.	89	D4
Carmen, Mex.	88	A1
Carnarvon, Aust.	100	A4
Caroline, is., Pac. Oc.	27	
Carpathian, mts., Europe	97	F4
Carpentaria, g., Arafura S.	100	C3
Carson City, Nevada	85	B3
Cartagena, Colombia	90	B1
Casablanca, Morocco	94	C2
Cascade Range, mts., U.S.A./Can.	86	A2
Casper, Wyoming, U.S.A.	85	C2
Caspian, s., Eur./Asia	96	J4
Caspian Depression, f., U.S.S.R.	97	H4
Cat, i., Bahama Is.	89	C2
Catoche, c., Mex.	87	G3
Caucasus, mts., U.S.S.R.	97	H4
Cayenne, Fr. Guiana	90	D2
Cedar Rapids, Iowa, U.S.A.	85	D2
Cedros, i., Pac. Oc.	87	A2
Celebes, i., Indonesia	98	G5
Celebes, s., Pac. Oc.	98	G4
Central African Republic, Africa	94	E5
Central Massif, f., France	97	D4
Central Plains, f., U.S.A.	86	E3
Central Russian Uplands, f., U.S.S.R.		
	97	G3
Central Siberian Plateau, f., U.S.S.R.		
	99	F1
Ceram, i., Indonesia	100	B2
Ceylon, see Sri Lanka	98	E4
Chad, Africa	94	E4
Chad, l., Africa	94	E4
Champlain, l., U.S.A./Can.	56	C5
Changchun, China	98	G2
Channel, is., English Ch.	96	C4
Chari, r., Chad/C.A.R.	94	E4
Charleston, S.C., U.S.A.	85	E3
Charleston, W. Virg., U.S.A.	85	E3
Charlotte, N.C., U.S.A.	85	E3
Chatham, is., Pac. Oc.	100	H6
Chatham, str., Alsk., U.S.A.	79	B1
Chattanooga, Tenn., U.S.A.	85	E3
Chelyuskin, c., U.S.S.R.	98	E1
Chesapeake, b., At. Oc.	86	F3
Chetumal, Mex.	88	B1
Chetumal, b., Carib. S.	88	B1
Cheyenne, Wyoming, U.S.A.	85	C2
Cheyenne, r., U.S.A.	86	C2
Chicago, Ill., U.S.A.	85	E2
Chichagof, i., Alsk., U.S.A.	79	B1
Chico, r., Argentina	90	C7
Chihuahua, Mex.	87	C2
Chile, S. Am.	90	B6
Chiloé, i., Chile	90	B7
China, Asia	98	F3
Chiriqui Lagoon, Panama	88	C3
Chonos, arch., Pac. Oc.	91	B7
Christchurch, N.Z.	100	G6
Christmas, i., Pac. Oc.	26	
Chukchi, s., Arc. Oc.	103	J2
Chungking, China	98	F3
Cienfuegos, Cuba	89	B2
Cimarron, r., U.S.A.	86	D3
Cincinnati, Ohio, U.S.A.	85	E3
Ciudad Juaréz, Mex.	87	C1
Ciudad Victoria, Mex.	87	E3
Cleveland, Ohio, U.S.A.	85	E2
Cloncurry, Aust.	100	D4
Coastal Plain, f., U.S.A.	86	E3
Coast Range, mts., U.S.A./Can.	86	A2
Cobán, Guatemala	88	A1
Cochabamba, Bolivia	90	C4
Cocos, is., Ind. Oc.	33	
Cod, c., Mass., U.S.A.	86	F2
Coiba, i., Pac. Oc.	88	C3
Cologne, Germany	96	D3
Colombia, S. Am.	90	B2
Colombo, Sri Lanka	98	E4
Colón, Panama	88	D3
Colorado, state, U.S.A.	85	C3
Colorado, r., Argentina	90	C6
Colorado, r., U.S.A.	86	D3
Colorado, r., U.S.A.	86	B3
Colorado Plateau, f., U.S.A.	86	B3
Columbia, S.C., U.S.A.	85	E3
Columbia, r., Canada/U.S.A.	86	A2
Columbus, Ohio, U.S.A.	85	E2
Comorin, c., India	98	D4
Comoro, is., Ind. Oc.	94	H7
Conakry, Guinea	94	B5
Concepción, Chile	90	B6
Concepción, Paraguay	90	D5
Conchos, r., Mex.	87	C2
Concord, N.H., U.S.A.	85	F2
Congo, bas., Africa	95	E5
Congo, r., Africa, see Zaïre, r.	94	E6
Congo Republic, Africa	94	E6
Connecticut, state, U.S.A.	85	F2
Connecticut, r., U.S.A.	84	
Cook, is., Pac. Oc.	26	
Cook, str., N.Z.	100	G6
Cooper's Creek, r., Aust.	100	D4
Copenhagen, Denmark	96	E3
Coral, s., Pac. Oc.	100	E3
Cordilleran Region, f., Canada/U.S.A.		
	35	E5
Córdoba, Argentina	90	C6
Corpus Christi, Tex., U.S.A.	87	E2
Corrientes, c., Mex.	87	C3
Corsica, i., Med. S.	96	D4
Costa Rica, C. Am.	88	C2
Crete, i., Med. S.	96	F5
Crooked, i., Bahama Is.	89	D2
Crozet, is., Ind. Oc.	27	
Cruz, c., Cuba	89	C3
Cuba, i., G. of Mex.	89	C2
Cubango, r., Africa	94	E7
Cuenca, Ecuador	90	B3
Curaçao, i., Carib. S.	89	E4
Curitiba, Brazil	90	E5
Cuzco, Peru	90	B4
Cyprus, i., Med. S.	96	G5
Czechoslovakia, Europe	96	E4
Dacca, Bangladesh	98	E3
Dahomey, see Benin	94	D5
Dakar, Senegal	94	B4
Dallas, Tex., U.S.A.	85	D3
Damascus, Syria	98	B3
Danube, r., Europe	96	E4
Dar es Salaam, Tanzania	94	G6
Darién, g., Carib. S.	91	B2
Darling, r., Aust.	100	D5
Darwin, Aust.	100	C3
David, Panama	88	C3
Davis, res. stat., Antarc.	102	D3
Davis, s., Ind. Oc.	102	E3
Daytona Beach, Fla., U.S.A.	85	E4
Dead, s., Israel/Jordan	96	G5
Delaware, state, U.S.A.	85	F3
Delaware, b., At. Oc.	86	F3
Delhi, India	98	D3
Denmark, Europe	96	D3
Denmark, str., Greenland/Iceland	34	J3
Denver, Colorado, U.S.A.	85	C3
Des Moines, Iowa, U.S.A.	85	D2
Detroit, Michigan, U.S.A.	85	E2
Detroit, r., Canada/U.S.A.	60	A3
Dinaric Alps, mts., Yugoslavia	97	E4
Djakarta, Indonesia	98	F5
Djibouti, Fr. Terr. of Afars & Issas	94	H4
Dnieper, r., U.S.S.R.	96	G4
Dniester, r., U.S.S.R.	96	F4
Dominica, i., Windward Is.	89	F3
Dominican Republic, Carib. S.	89	D3
Don, r., U.S.S.R.	96	H4
Donetsk, U.S.S.R.	96	G4
Douala, Cameroon	94	D5
Dover, Delaware, U.S.A.	85	F3
Drakensberg, mts., S. Africa	95	F9

Name	Page	Grid
Honduras, C. Am.	88	B2
Honduras, g., Carib. S.	88	B1
Hong Kong, Asia	98	F3
Honolulu, Hawaiian Is.	32	
Honshu, i., Japan	98	G3
Horn, c., Chile	90	C8
Hot Springs, Arkansas, U.S.A.	85	D3
Houston, Tex., U.S.A.	85	D4
Howe, c., Aust.	100	E5
Huambo (Nova Lisboa), Angola	94	E7
Hudson, r., U.S.A.	86	F2
Humboldt (Peru), cur., Pac. Oc.	93	A3
Humboldt, r., U.S.A.	86	B2
Hungary, Europe	96	E4
Huron, l., Canada/U.S.A.	85	E2
Hwang, r., China	98	F3
Hyderabad, India	98	D4
Ibadan, Nigeria	94	D5
Iberian, pen., Europe	97	C4
Iceland, i., At. Oc.	34	K3
Idaho, state, U.S.A.	85	B2
Idaho Falls, Idaho, U.S.A.	85	B2
Illinois, state, U.S.A.	85	E2
Illinois, r., U.S.A.	86	E2
India, Asia	98	D4
Indiana, state, U.S.A.	85	E2
Indianapolis, Indiana, U.S.A.	85	E3
Indian Ocean	27	
Indigirka, r., U.S.S.R.	98	H1
Indonesia, Asia	98	F5
Indus, r., Pakistan	98	D3
Ionian, s., Med. S.	96	E5
Iowa, state, U.S.A.	85	D2
Ipswich, Aust.	100	E4
Iquique, Chile	90	B5
Iran, Asia	98	C3
Iraq, Asia	98	C3
Ireland, Europe	96	C3
Irish, s., At. Oc.	96	C3
Irrawaddy, r., Burma	98	E3
Irtysh, r., U.S.S.R.	98	D2
Ishim, r., U.S.S.R.	98	D2
Islamabad, Pakistan	98	D3
Isle Royale, i., Mich., U.S.A.	66	C3
Israel, Asia	98	B3
Istanbul, Turkey	96	F4
Italy, Europe	96	E4
Ivory Coast, Africa	94	C5
Izmir, Turkey	96	F5
Jackson, Miss., U.S.A.	85	D3
Jacksonville, Florida, U.S.A.	85	E3
Jacmel, Haiti	89	D3
Jalapa, Mex.	87	E4
Jamaica, ch., Jamaica/Haiti	89	D3
Jamaica, i., Carib. S.	89	C3
Japan, is., Asia	98	G3
Japan, s., Pac. Oc.	98	G2
Java, i., Indonesia	98	F5
Java, s., Pac. Oc.	99	F5
Jefferson City, Missouri, U.S.A.	85	D3
Jerusalem, Israel/Jordan	98	B3
Johannesburg, Rep. of S. Africa	94	F8
Jordan, Asia	98	B3
Joseph Bonaparte, g., Timor S.	100	B3
Juan Fernandez, i., Pac. Oc.	90	B6
Juneau, Alsk., U.S.A.	79	B1
Juticalpa, Hon.	90	B2
Kabul, Afghanistan	98	D3
Kaiser Wilhelm II Land, Antarc.	102	E3
Kalahari, des., Africa	95	F8
Kalgoorlie, Aust.	100	B5
Kalimantan (Borneo), Indonesia	98	F5
Kamchatka, pen., U.S.S.R.	99	J2
Kampala, Uganda	94	G5
Kangaroo, i., Aust.	100	C5
Kano, Nigeria	94	D4
Kanpur, India	98	E3
Kansas, state, U.S.A.	85	D3
Kansas, r., U.S.A.	86	D3
Kansas City, Kansas, U.S.A.	85	D3
Kara, s., Arc. Oc.	98	D1
Karachi, Pakistan	98	D3
Kasai, r., Zaïre/Angola	94	E6
Kasanga, Tanzania	94	G6
Kashmir, India/Pak.	98	D3
Katmandu, Nepal	98	E3
Kattegat, str., Den./Sweden	96	E3
Kemp Land, Antarc.	102	C3
Kentucky, state, U.S.A.	85	E3
Kenya, Africa	94	G5
Kerguelen, i., Ind. Oc.	27	
Keweenaw, b., L. Superior	66	C3
Keweenaw, pt., Mich., U.S.A.	66	C3
Key West, Fla., U.S.A.	89	B2
Khangai, mts., Asia	99	E2
Kharkov, U.S.S.R.	96	G3
Khartoum, Sudan	94	G4
Khmer Republic, see Cambodia	98	F4
Kiev, U.S.S.R.	96	G3
Kigali, Rwanda	94	G6
Kimberley, Rep. of S. Africa	94	F8
Kingston, Jamaica	89	C3
Kingstown, St. Vincent	89	F4
Kinshasa, Zaïre	94	E6
Kirgiz Steppe, f., U.S.S.R.	99	D2
Kisangani, Zaïre	94	F5
Kismayu, Somali Rep.	94	H6
Kivu, l., Zaïre/Rwanda	94	F6
Knoxville, Tenn., U.S.A.	85	E3
Kolyma, r., U.S.S.R.	98	H1
Korea, Asia	98	G3
Kota Kinabalu, Sabah	98	F4
Kuala Lumpur, Malaysia	98	F4
Kuching, Sarawak	98	F4
Kunlun Shan, mts., Asia	99	E3
Kupreanof, i., Alsk., U.S.A.	79	B1
Kuril, is., Pac. Oc.	98	H2
Kuwait, Asia	98	C3
Kyoto, Japan	98	G3
Kyushu, i., Japan	98	G3
Labrador, cur., At. Oc.	37	H4
Laccadive, is., Ind. Oc.	98	D4
La Ceiba, Hon.	88	B1
Ladoga, l., U.S.S.R.	96	G2
Lagos, Nigeria	94	D5
Lahore, Pakistan	98	D3
Land's End, c., England	96	C3
Lansing, Mich., U.S.A.	85	E2
Laos, Asia	98	F4
La Paz, Bolivia	90	C4
La Paz, Mex.	87	B3
Lapland, Europe	97	F2
La Plata, Argentina	90	D6
Laptev, s., Arc. Oc.	103	M2
Las Palmas, Canary Is.	94	B3
Las Vegas, Nevada, U.S.A.	85	B3
Latvia, rep., U.S.S.R.	96	F3
Lazarev, res. stat., Antarc.	102	A2
Lebanon, Asia	98	B3
Leeuwin, c., Aust.	100	A5
Leeward, is., Carib. S.	89	F3
Lena, r., U.S.S.R.	98	G1
Leningrad, U.S.S.R.	96	G2
León, Mex.	87	D3
León, Nic.	88	B2
Lesotho, Africa	94	F8
Lesser Antilles, is., Carib. S.	89	F4
Lhasa, Tibet	98	E3
Liberia, Africa	94	C5
Libreville, Gabon	94	D5
Libya, Africa	94	E3
Libyan, plateau, Africa	95	F2
Libyan, des., Africa	95	F3
Liechtenstein, Europe	96	D4
Lima, Peru	90	B4
Limón, Costa Rica	88	C3
Limpopo, r., Africa	94	F8
Lincoln, Neb., U.S.A.	85	D2
Lions, g., Med. S.	96	D4
Lisbon, Portugal	96	C5
Lithuania, rep., U.S.S.R.	96	F3
Little America, res. stat., Antarc.	102	L2
Little Miquelon, i., At. Oc.	48	C4
Little Rock, Arkansas, U.S.A.	85	D3
Liverpool, England	96	C3
Llanos, f., S. Am.	91	C2
Lódź, Poland	96	E3
Loire, r., France	96	C4
Lombok, i., Indonesia	100	A2
Lomé, Togo	94	D5
London, England	96	C3
Londonderry, c., Aust.	100	B3
Long, i., Bahama Is.	89	C2
Long, i., N.Y., U.S.A.	86	F2
Lopatka, c., U.S.S.R.	98	H2
Los Angeles, Calif., U.S.A.	85	B3
Louisiana, state, U.S.A.	85	D3
Louisville, Kentucky, U.S.A.	85	E3
Lourenço Marques, see Can Phumo	94	G8
Lower California, reg., Mex.	87	B2
Loyalty, is., Pac. Oc.	100	F4
Lualaba, r., Zaïre	94	F6
Luanda, Angola	94	E6
Lubumbashi, Zaïre	94	F7
Lusaka, Zambia	94	F7
Lüta, China	98	G3
Lützow-Holm, b., Ind. Oc.	102	B3
Luxembourg, Europe	96	D4
Luzon, i., Philippines	98	G4
Lyons, France	96	D4
Macao, Asia	98	F3
Macassar, Indonesia	100	A2
Macassar, str., Borneo/Celebes	98	F5
Macdonnell Range, mts., Aust.	101	C4
Maceió, Brazil	90	F3
Macías Nguema, i., Gulf of Guinea	94	D5
Macquarie, i., Pac. Oc.	33	
Mac-Robertson Land, Antarc.	102	D3
Madagascar, Africa	95	H7
Madeira, i., At. Oc.	94	B2
Madeira, r., S. Am.	90	C3
Madison, Wisconsin, U.S.A.	85	E2
Madras, India	98	E4
Madrid, Spain	96	C4

CANADA
40-84

NORTH
AMERICA
34-39

UNITED STATES
85,86

THE
CARIBBEAN
ISLANDS
89

MEXICO
87

CENTRAL
AMERICA
88

SOUTH
AMERICA
90-93

THE WORLD
26-33